Simple, Fresh & Healthy

Simple, Fresh & Healthy

A Collection of Seasonal Recipes

by Linda Hafner
of Chuck Hafner's Farmer's Market

with Denise Owen Harrigan
Photography by James Scherzi
Design by Holly Boice Scherzi

BEAUFORT
BOOKS
NEW YORK

FIRST EDITION

Library of Congress Cataloging-in-Publication Data

Hafner, Linda.
Simple, fresh & healthy / Linda Hafner.
p. cm.
Includes bibliographical references and index.
ISBN 978-0-8253-0557-3 (alk. paper)
1. Cooking (Vegetables) 2. Cooking (Fruit) I. Title. II. Title: Simple, fresh, and healthy.
TX801.H24 2011
641.6'5--dc22
2010031945

For inquiries about volume orders, please contact:

Beaufort Books
27 West 20th Street, Suite 1102
New York, NY 10011
sales@beaufortbooks.com

Published in the United States by Beaufort Books
www.beaufortbooks.com

Distributed by Midpoint Trade Books
www.midpointtrade.com

Cover and book design by Holly Boice Scherzi

Printed in China.

This book is dedicated to my family:

My husband, Chuck, for his love and support for the last 40 years.

My three children, Jess, Ryan, and Taryn, who have brought more joy into my life than I ever imagined possible.

To my Mom for inspiring my love of cooking fresh, simple, delicious food. (I still strive to cook as well as you do, Mom.)

To my Dad, who told me I could learn to do whatever I wanted to do.

To the Hafner and Gelsomin families — I am blessed to have you all in my life.

Finally, to my first grandchild, Patrick, may you thrive and grow strong eating Simple, Fresh, and Healthy food!

Acknowledgments

I want to thank Jim and Holly for believing in my book concept right from the start . . . and for making it a reality. I especially thank Jim for keeping me calm and Holly, for being the essence of calm. And thank you, Katelyn for keeping thousands of photo files in meticulous order.

I want to thank Denny for listening to me talk about my cooking philosophy and for so beautifully translating my ideas into words. My daughters both think you've captured me to a "T."

To Jess, Ryan, and Taryn, who encouraged me for years to write a cookbook. Thank you, thank you . . . I finally did it!

Thanks also to my sister, Janet, for her advice and for testing recipes. And thanks to my sister Ann (who is also a dietician) and to my brothers, George and Tom, for our endless, and always inspiring, conversations about food and recipes.

Many, many thanks to my cousin Maria for analyzing the recipes with so much care and precision.

To Sam Tassone, thanks for allowing us to photograph your beautiful crops on your picture-perfect farm.

A big thank you to all of our employees for all of their enthusiasm for this book.

And to all my special friends — you know who you are — thank you for always being there.

Linda and Chuck Hafner

Foreword

As a Registered Dietitian, I have spent my career encouraging people to eat healthfully. In my early days, I studied the work of Ancel Keys and his Seven Countries Study. His research proved that the Mediterranean diet was the healthiest on earth. More than 50 years later we now know you don't have to live in the Mediterranean to reap the benefits. Eating a diet that includes whole grains, fish, beans, nuts, seeds, fresh herbs, extra virgin olive oil, and locally grown produce at the peak of ripeness is the key. I always marveled at the European way of eating in the seasons, and filling the plate with an abundance of fruits and vegetables. This concept is gaining favor in the United States, but many Americans struggle to make it a reality. Linda's book is a testament to healthy, natural eating. She has taken tried and true family recipes that are not only delectably delicious but easy to prepare. This book will capture your senses with its brilliant photography and please your palate with the simple fresh taste of food from the earth. As she takes you through the seasons on this culinary adventure, you will realize how great healthy eating makes you feel. The key to good health is not found on some tropical island or far away hilltop, but is literally right in your back yard.

Linda J. Quinn, MS, RD

Linda Quinn, MS, RD, CDN
Distinguished Dietitian of the Year, New York State Dietetic Association, Spokesperson for New York Apple Association (www.nyapplecountry.com), Writer, Columnist and TV Dietitian.

The Disappearing Dinner Hour:
A Cause Worth Saving

By Linda Hafner

Growing up in my mother's buzzing beehive of a kitchen, I could never have imagined that a kitchen could be silent or that cooking could become an endangered art. The kitchen is the heart of the home. Home cooking is the core of family life, not to mention the foundation of good health. What could be more obvious?

In retrospect, I was naïve about how rapidly life can change. By the time our first child was born in 1975, I was seeing signs of a culture shift. At the farm stand, we gradually stopped selling produce by the bushel as customers lost interest in pickling and canning. More women, many of them wives and mothers, were entering the workforce. Computers became increasingly common, and then indispensable. But instead of simplifying life, computers seemed to quicken its pace. We had more to accomplish and less time in which to do it.

Even our children seemed pressured. Instead of playing in the yard after school, they had music and gymnastics lessons, swim meets and soccer practice. Instead of playing ball in the park down the street, they played across town (if not out-of-town). Parents who were fortunate enough to be home with their kids were most likely to be on the road, chauffeuring them to lessons and games.

While our economy grew — and our children grew more accomplished — this hectic new lifestyle took its toll, especially in the American kitchen. We became a nation on the run, and in our race to do it all, the once-essential (and enjoyable) art of cooking seemed to slip away. In its place came a parade of modern meal options, with no connection to our kitchens: fast food, take-out food, microwave dinners, and pizza delivered to our doorstep.

My own family was by no means immune to these changes. I always worked in our growing family business beside my husband, Chuck. But I was fortunate to control my own schedule, so I was usually home after school. Even though our children's schedules sometimes made me dizzy, I was known in the neighborhood as the mother who always had something cooking.

I did it as much for my inner peace as for my family. I kept cooking because I'm Italian and hardwired to feed people. Cooking, for us, is as natural as breathing. Perhaps I kept cooking because Chuck and I settled so close to our families, and their lives revolved around growing and cooking food. Even today, my parents, now in their 80s, have a garden that's larger than my house and a freezer with enough homemade food for a complete church supper.

After growing up with food that was so fresh, healthy, and delicious, I never saw the point of fast food. Why eat processed, mass-produced food when fresh, home-cooked meals taste so much better?

It's not that I lived in a bubble. Like the rest of my generation, I was always busy: growing a business and raising a family. But when I was first married, I learned a crucial lesson. Chuck and I often worked 12-hour days at the farm stand. When I didn't eat properly, I couldn't keep up with the work. Skipping meals — then grabbing a brownie for instant energy — quickly backfired. On empty calories, I couldn't carry bushels of tomatoes or stock the farm stand.

When our children came along, the importance of healthy food took on new urgency. At first, I was a little obsessed. I made baby food, bread, and yogurt from scratch. But as the demands on my time grew, I had to be realistic. This is when my Simple, Fresh & Healthy mantra became crystal clear. It was my roadmap for continuing to cook, without compromising on ingredients — or collapsing in an exhausted heap. Often my quick meals featured the fresh produce I brought home from the farm stand or from my father's garden.

Instead of depleting my energy, cooking gives me energy to spare. I thrive on the same healthy food I feed to my family. I also unwind as I cook. After a whirlwind day, peeling, chopping, and stirring settle me down. Best of all, cooking is a very social experience. For centuries, families and friends have congregated in kitchens. Some of my favorite moments as a mother have taken place in my kitchen, with my kids doing homework on one side of the counter and me chopping away on the other. We'd catch up on the day's news and nibble on fresh fruit and vegetables. And I'd always have a ready answer to that eternal question, "Mom, what's for dinner?"

Now that my daughters are married and living in other states, I love going to their homes, working beside them in their kitchens, and exchanging recipes. I still love helping my mother and my sisters prepare our favorite holiday dishes. I love working on the cooking teams that feed the Hafner brood — now 55 strong — when we gather at weeklong family reunions.

I don't think I need to a make a case for the health benefits of fresh food. As a nation, we are finally waking up to the nutritional consequences of fast or processed food, especially those items that are high in fat and sugar. So I won't be preaching about nutrition in this book, simply making it easier to serve healthy, delicious meals. That said, here are a few things I've learned:

Less Is More

When I visited Italy with my grandmother, I felt immediately at home with the Italian approach to cooking, which, coincidentally, *is* simple, fresh, and healthy. The Italians feasted on fresh vegetables, often mixing them with pasta. They proudly set out prized local products like thinly sliced prosciutto and fresh mozzarella cheese. They finished their meals with fresh fruit. They savored every bite, and lingered at the table for hours, laughing and telling stories. Italians understand that good food nourishes the body, and good company nourishes the soul.

Go For It!

While I often reduce the amount of sugar or fat in everyday recipes, I'm not opposed to splurging with special occasion or traditional family favorites, such as my mother's meatballs or my family's chocolate birthday cake. A steady diet of deprivation can lead to obsession. If most of what you eat is healthy, you've earned an occasional treat. Enjoy.

Taste As You Go

Many ingredients — especially fresh ingredients — vary in taste and texture from season to season, even from day to day. It's a good idea to taste as you cook, so you can adjust seasonings or cooking times. With my Apple Country Cake, for instance, I increase the amount of sugar when I make it with tart, early-season apples.

Make Salad a Staple

At our house, I serve a green salad at the end of the evening meal. It's an Italian custom, supposedly to aid digestion. But *when* you eat your salad is not crucial — as long as you eat those fresh, raw greens every day.

Keep Fruit Center Stage

Eating fresh fruit is a habit worth cultivating. I always keep a plate of fresh, washed fruit on the kitchen counter, so it's the first thing to tempt us when we reach for a snack.

Divide and Conquer

At the end of the day, I rarely have time to cook a full meal. But I can usually find a few minutes here and there (even the night before) to tackle a little prep work, such as cleaning greens, chopping onions, peeling potatoes, or blanching vegetables. Even a special occasion recipe with multiple steps — such as my Fruit Pizza — can be accomplished in small painless increments.

Improvise!

I encourage you to be creative with my recipes. You can usually substitute different vegetables, fruits, herbs, and seasonings according to what you have on hand. One note of caution: baking tends to be more scientific than cooking, so it pays to be precise. While you can substitute strawberries for the peaches in my Perfect Peach Shortcake, you'll want to use the exact ingredients listed for the biscuits.

Make Cooking a Team Sport

My father always said he didn't need a dishwasher, because he already had three — my two sisters and myself. We all served our time in the kitchen. Today, there's no place we'd rather be. Whether it's shopping, chopping, cooking, or cleaning up, involve your family. Someday, they'll thank you.

Ryan, Taryn and Jess

The Hafner Way

When I married Chuck Hafner in the spring of 1971, I must confess to an ulterior motive: first pick of the fresh fruits and vegetables from his family's legendary farm in North Syracuse. While I certainly married for love — Chuck was my childhood sweetheart — the field-fresh strawberries, corn, and tomatoes helped seal the deal.

At the time, I was a home economics teacher, at ease in the kitchen and an early believer in nutrition. I was also a grocer's daughter. My parents were the lovebirds behind another North Syracuse landmark, Sweetheart Market. But my passion for fresh produce is probably genetic — encoded by generations of Italian ancestors who built their lives around fresh, simple food.

Those Italian traditions followed my family all the way to North Syracuse. Our house was surrounded by fruit trees, berry patches, vegetable gardens — even an asparagus bed. Like most Italian families, our lives (certainly our conversations) revolved around what we were growing, cooking, baking, canning, or consuming.

Chuck's childhood also revolved around fresh fruits and vegetables, but on a much larger scale. During college, Chuck spent his summers working at the family farm. He graduated with a political science degree but soon realized he could earn a better living selling produce (a seasonal venture that left plenty of time for his winter passion: skiing).

To sync our careers (and free our winters for travel), I left teaching and worked with Chuck at the farm stand — a

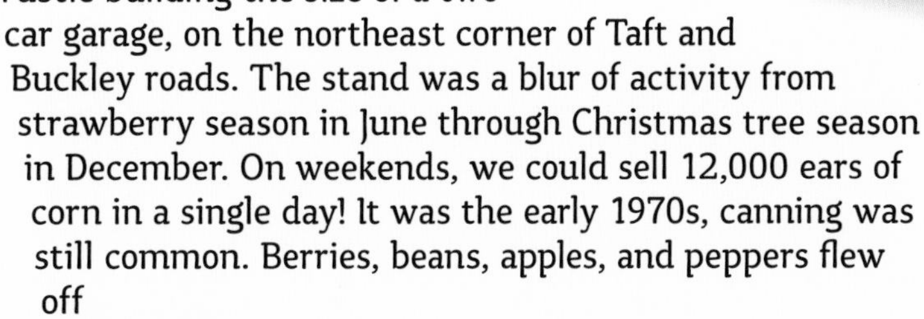

rustic building the size of a two-car garage, on the northeast corner of Taft and Buckley roads. The stand was a blur of activity from strawberry season in June through Christmas tree season in December. On weekends, we could sell 12,000 ears of corn in a single day! It was the early 1970s, canning was still common. Berries, beans, apples, and peppers flew off the shelves.

But gradually we saw a shift in our business. Customers grew more and more interested in planting flowers and trees. We turned the farm stand into an ice cream stand and built a farm market and garden center next door. We continued to sell plenty of seasonal produce, but our growth — and boy, did we grow, right along with our three children, born in 1975, 1976, and 1981 — was in our greenhouses, where every year we nudged hundreds of thousands of plants toward bloom.

In 2009, we reached a major milestone, moving our business across Buckley Road into a 65,000 square-foot retail complex with seven state-of-the-art greenhouses, custom-built and shipped here from Holland. We now have room to grow — literally — with plenty of space for a café, an ice cream stand, and, of course, fresh produce.

With all the changes we have witnessed in our growing business and growing family — not to mention in our culture — the constant in my life has been cooking meals that are fresh, simple, and delicious. The same vibrant fruits and vegetables you see in our produce section are likely to be starring in our family dinner.

I can't take much credit for cooking: as I said, I am hardwired to cook, courtesy of my Italian family. But I largely attribute my good health, and my family's good health, to the simple practice of cooking with food that is fresh and in season.

My cooking style is not complicated. My recipes rarely require exotic ingredients or hours of preparation. I usually spend about 30 to 45 minutes creating a dinner that typically includes a main course, vegetable, fresh salad, and fruit. I may start dinner before I leave for work in the morning. More often than not, I peel, chop, cook, and clean up while chatting (and ideally sipping wine) with friends and family.

The purpose of this book is to encourage others (especially the younger generation) to join this close-knit, high-dividend circle. Invest a little time in creating fresh, simple meals. The process of cooking centers you. It grounds your family. It fuels a lifetime of good health. (My parents, I am happy to report, are well into their 80s, still strong, sharp and energetic — and still gardening and cooking for their five children, 12 grandchildren, and 4 great-grandchildren.)

May you and your family likewise learn to love — and to thrive on — the fresh, nutritious, and delicious ingredients that grow around us.

Linda

Linda Hafner

Photo at right:
My mother's hands
chopping vegetables, as usual.

Hafner Family History

The Hafner family hails from Stuttgart, Germany. In 1908, Louis and Christine Hafner immigrated to America with their four children in tow. The oldest child, Louis Jr., was the ripe age of 5 years, and the youngest, Mary, was a mere 3 months. Without much room in between, were sons George, 4, and Jacob, 2. Nothing like immigrating to a new country with four toddlers!

The family established a home in North Syracuse, N.Y. at the corner of Allen and Taft roads and began farming the land. Sadly, in 1920, 12 years after settling in upstate N.Y., Louis Hafner passed away. Four years later, his son, Louis Jr., 21, also died. That left George, 20, and Jacob, 18, to run the family farm, with Mom as boss.

George and Jake (as he became known) sold their produce at the Regional Farmers Market and to local supermarkets. During harvest season, they set up tables in front of their house. Workers traveling along Taft Road would stop by to pick up fresh strawberries, corn, tomatoes, etc.

In 1935, George fell in love and married a beautiful woman from Eastwood named Katherine Hoffman. They had four children: Joan, Barbara, Patricia, and Chuck. Jake also fell in love and married the lovely Mary Dwyer, from Syracuse's west side, in 1938. In Hafner family tradition, they too had four children: Peter, Heidi, Tom, and Mike. Speaking of tradition, all children were expected to work on the farm, in the strawberry fields, and at the Regional Market.

The farm became known as Hafner Brothers and operated as such until George and Jake were in their 60s. In the farm's heyday, the brothers worked approximately 185 acres, farming asparagus, strawberries, raspberries, tomatoes, string beans, peppers, and squash, to name a few. The plants were started in their small greenhouses, tended mainly by Jake. The crops were then planted in rows marked by George walking behind one of his Percheron horses.

In 1968, traffic on West Taft Road became so heavy that the county had to widen the road. George and Kate's home was now so close to the street, they moved it back to Buckley Road. George and his son, Chuck, then constructed a building that was about the size of a two-car garage. This was the beginning of Chuck Hafner's Farmer's Market, although, you may be more familiar with it as an ice cream stand.

In 1971, Chuck married his high-school sweetheart, Linda Gelsomin. Linda, a teacher at the time, left teaching to help Chuck with their business. (It may have had something to do with the fact that teachers have the summer off and farmers have the winter off.)

Linda also comes from a family business. One mile east of Chuck and Linda's stand is The Sweetheart Corner, named after Linda's "lovebird" parents. They started their business in 1947 as Sweetheart Ice Cream, which later transformed into Sweetheart Market. George and Lee, together with their family, maintained Sweetheart Market until 2003.

In 1975, Chuck and Linda built what their family fondly calls "the stand," and began selling nursery, flowers, and gardening supplies along with homegrown produce. Also, Chuck and Linda's first child, Jess, was born, and sister, Ryan, arrived the following summer of 1976.

Sadly, in the fall of 1980, the family lost George Hafner. But in January 1981, Chuck and Linda's third child, Taryn, was born. True to Hafner tradition, Jess, Ryan, and Taryn all spent time helping out at the family business — especially Jess, who continues to work alongside his father creating new vision and growth in the business.

-Taryn Hafner Hullsiek

George Hafner

Digging In: Linda's First Garden

I have a confession to make. Until I created this cookbook, I had never grown a vegetable from seed to harvest. Technically, I have gardening credentials galore. I grew up working in my grandfather's garden, where my favorite task was tying cauliflower leaves together, to keep the heads snowy white.

For the past 40 years, I have worked beside my husband, Chuck, growing our family business into one of Central New York's largest garden centers/farm markets. I have planted, nurtured, and watered more vegetable and flower seedlings than I can count. I have sold thousands of bushels of fresh-picked corn, tomatoes, and cucumbers. And I have grown plenty of fresh herbs and potted tomatoes on my patio, just steps from my kitchen.

But until this cookbook took shape, I had never planted, watered, weeded, fussed and fretted over my very own vegetable patch.

Once I decided to dig in, it was remarkably easy. We framed a 6-by-10 foot raised-bed garden in a well-traveled section of the nursery yard. We filled it with a rich mixture of topsoil and Chuck's compost, then planted the tiny seedlings in tidy rows.

Week 1

From there it was a simple matter of daily watering, a little weeding, and lots of admiring the fast-growing greenery. Five weeks after planting, I harvested my first crop of curly spinach leaves. Maybe I'm biased, but it was the tastiest, most tender spinach I've ever eaten.

Growing my own vegetables, from start to finish, has turned out to be one of the easiest and most gratifying experiences of my life. I guess it's like the difference between admiring someone else's baby and having your own. It's magical. I finally understand that sparkle in my father's eye, when I find him in his garden.

My Dad in his asparagus garden.

1. pole beans
2. tomatoes (Grape)
3. tomatoes ("Mountain Pride")
4. tomatoes ("Early Girl")
5. rhubarb
6. bush cucumber
7. green pepper
8. carrots
9. broccoli
10. zuchinni
11. herbs (clockwise)
    a. rosemary
    b. Italian parsley
    c. basil
    d. nasturtium
12. spinach
13. spinach - leaf lettuce
14. leaf lettuce
15. romaine

Week 3

Week 6

Spring: The Tender Season

When the first green shoots of spring peek through our frozen Central New York soil, we welcome them like long-lost friends. Winter may be slow to release its grip, but spring is finally flexing its slender fingers. Vibrant flowers, fruits, and vegetables will soon follow. What better reward for enduring a hard Central New York winter?

At Chuck Hafner's Garden Center, we jump-start spring in the dead of winter, planting tens of thousands of flowers and vegetables. Even in our new greenhouses, growing healthy, hardy plants (worthy of the Hafner name) depends mightily on the human touch. It's a labor-intensive, time-consuming process, making spring our busiest season by far. In fact, we do 40 percent of our annual business in the month of May.

You might think that all this activity would keep me out of the kitchen. But the busier I am, the more important cooking becomes. Hard work requires good fuel; and fresh food, simply prepared, makes the best fuel. Just ask my husband, Chuck. One typical spring day, we hooked him up to a pedometer. He clocked 15 miles walking around our greenhouses and nursery yards. You don't get that kind of steady energy from fast or processed food.

But I also cook because cooking centers me. And spring's procession of home-grown delicacies thrills me — from the first slender stalk of April asparagus to the last juicy, local strawberry. After a long winter of stews and root vegetables, I can't wait to share these precious tastes of spring.

Spring

Asparagus

- To begin growing asparagus requires patience. Approximate time between planting crowns and regular cutting is two years.
- Once asparagus gets established, patience is no longer required. It is one of the first vegetables harvested in spring.
- The choice of thin or thick spears, though much argued, is purely a matter of preference.
- Asparagus prefers a sandy soil with good drainage — its feet don't like to be wet.
- Give asparagus plenty of room to grow — a mature plant will yield about 20-25 spears.
- Asparagus lovers enjoy a harvest period of about six weeks; cutting should stop about mid-June.
- When purchasing, look for tips that are closed.

Fresh, Simple, Healthy Recipe

Steamed Asparagus with Lemon

1 pound of fresh, locally grown asparagus, washed
water for cooking
salt and pepper to taste
a squeeze of lemon juice or 1 tsp of fresh lemon zest (optional)
1 T olive oil

- Bring an inch of water to a boil in an asparagus cooker or a pot that is tall enough to allow the stalks to stand upright.
- Trim the asparagus. Hold one end of the spear in each hand and bend; the spear will naturally break at the point where it becomes tough.
- Place asparagus — tips up — in pot and steam 5-10 minutes until crisp-tender.
- Drain. Salt and pepper to taste. Add the olive oil and a splash of lemon juice, or lemon zest if desired.

[It's best to cook asparagus upright — most of the nutrients are in the tip and won't be lost in the cooking water. Asparagus is loaded with folic acid, A and B vitamins, and fiber.]

Serves 4. Each serving supplies:
Calories(kcal) 42 Protein 1(g) Carbohydrates 3(g) Dietary Fiber 1(g) Cholesterol 0(mg) Fat 3(g) Sodium 1(mg)

Asparagus Frittata

This is my definition of soul food. Essentially an Italian omelet, the rustic frittata transforms spring's tender asparagus spears into a meal. In May, when we're crazy-busy at the Garden Center, my mother will call to say she's made this frittata for our lunch, using fresh asparagus from my father's backyard patch.

1 pound **fresh asparagus spears**

¼ cup **onion**, minced

6 **eggs**

¼ cup **grated cheese** (Romano or Locatelli)

1 T **olive oil**

Salt and pepper to taste

- Wash, trim, and cut asparagus into 1-inch pieces.
- Add oil to an 8-inch, nonstick frying pan and place over medium-high heat. Add asparagus, cover, and cook for about 3 minutes, stirring occasionally. Add onion and continue to cook until crisp-tender, 3-5 minutes longer. Season to taste with salt and pepper.
- Meanwhile, whisk together the eggs, grated cheese, salt, and pepper. Pour mixture into frying pan, stirring to distribute the asparagus. Cook over medium-high heat, stirring frequently, until eggs are quite firm and hold together — about 5-6 minutes.
- Remove from heat and set a plate, face down, over the top of the frying pan. Carefully flip the frittata onto the plate and slide it back into the frying pan. Cook another minute or two. Slip the finished frittata onto a serving plate. Serve warm or at room temperature.

Serves 6. Each serving supplies:
Calories(kcal) 120 Protein 8(g) Carbohydrates 3(g) Dietary Fiber 1(g)
Cholesterol 214(mg) Fat 9(g) Sodium 151(mg)

Fusilli with Chicken, Asparagus, and Tomatoes

A symphony of flavors, colors, and textures, this easy spring supper is actually a dish for all seasons, since asparagus and grape tomatoes are not only available but quite flavorful most of the year. But I still recommend using our sublime Central New York asparagus if it's in season. It practically sings spring!

8 ounces **fusilli pasta**, uncooked

1 T **olive oil**

1 pound **skinless, boneless chicken breast**, finely cut into ¼-inch strips

½ tsp **salt**

½ tsp freshly ground **black pepper**

1 cup sliced **asparagus**, in 1-inch pieces, uncooked

2 cups **grape tomatoes**, halved

2 **garlic cloves**, minced

2 T chopped **fresh basil**

2 T **white balsamic vinegar**

1 T **extra virgin olive oil**

¼ cup **crumbled goat cheese**

- Prepare fusilli according to package directions, timing it so that pasta is ready to drain when chicken and vegetables are cooked.
- Sprinkle chicken strips with salt and pepper. Heat 1 tablespoon olive oil in a large nonstick skillet over medium-high heat. Add chicken and asparagus and sauté for 5 minutes.
- Add tomatoes and garlic. Sauté for 1 minute and remove from heat.
- Drain cooked pasta and add to skillet. Stir in basil, vinegar, and extra virgin olive oil. Divide into four portions and garnish each with a tablespoon of cheese. This recipe is best cold or at room temperature.

Serves 4. Each serving supplies:

Calories(kcal) 438 Protein 36(g) Carbohydrates 49(g) Dietary Fiber 4(g) Cholesterol 72(mg) Fat 11(g) Sodium 406(mg)

[When draining pasta, reserve a cup of cooking water. Add a little at a time if the final mixture seems too dry.]

Spinach

- Synonymous with spring in Central New York, spinach grows rapidly and can be harvested early.
- Widely considered the world's most nutritious vegetable, it's been shown to enhance brain function – and to fight cancer, heart disease, and inflammation.
- Avoid bruised and wilted leaves; smaller, younger leaves are more delicate.
- A serving of steamed spinach makes a healthy, tasty bed for fish, chicken, beef, or pork.

Fresh, Simple, Healthy Recipe

Steamed Spinach

1 pound **spinach**

2 **garlic cloves**, halved

1-2 tsp **olive oil**

Salt and pepper to taste

Serves 4. Each serving supplies:
Calories(kcal) 36 Protein 2(g) Carbohydrates 3(g) Dietary Fiber 2(g) Cholesterol 0(mg) Fat 2(g) Sodium 65(mg)

- Remove stem ends and imperfect leaves. Wash leaves thoroughly to remove dirt that can settle into leaves. Rinse but do not dry.
- Place spinach leaves in a medium saucepan and place over medium heat. Cover and cook for 3-5 minutes, until the leaves are wilted and tender.
- Drain any remaining water, if necessary. Add the garlic and gently toss the spinach with olive oil. Season with salt and pepper.

The last-minute addition of garlic infuses the spinach with subtle flavor – but you might want to remove the cloves before serving.

Linda's Garden
Soil Mix

Spinach and Strawberry Salad

With strawberries practically in our genes, the Hafner family can never get enough of these sweet ruby jewels. I love the idea of introducing strawberries into a savory salad, especially when you add creamy cheese and crunchy walnuts to this colorful mix.

Salad

8 cups baby spinach leaves, washed and dried (or mixture of spinach and torn romaine leaves)

¼ cup Vidalia onion, thinly sliced

2 cups strawberries, washed and sliced

1 cup fresh mozzarella, cubed

Dressing

¼ cup olive oil

2 T white balsamic vinegar

2 T orange juice

1 tsp honey

salt and pepper to taste

⅓ cup chopped walnuts or sliced almonds

- In a small bowl, whisk together dressing ingredients. (Dressing will keep covered in refrigerator for two days.)
- In a salad bowl, combine the spinach, onion, strawberries, and mozzarella. Drizzle with dressing and toss gently.
- Sprinkle with nuts and serve immediately.

Serves 4. Each serving supplies:
Calories(kcal) 345 Protein 9(g) Carbohydrates 19(g) Dietary Fiber 5(g) Cholesterol 23(mg) Fat 27(g) Sodium 178(mg)

Baked Haddock with Spinach and Cheese Sauce

In Italy, where spinach is also a spring staple, a dish that's cooked on a bed of spinach and gilded with a rich sauce is called "a la Florentine." My version is rich in taste but much lower in calories, thanks to low-fat milk and very flavorful Parmesan cheese.

1 tsp grated **lemon zest**

1¾ cup **1% milk**

3 T **flour**

½ cup plus 2 T **freshly grated Parmesan cheese**

Freshly ground pepper

Cayenne pepper to taste

1 pound **fresh spinach**

1 pound **haddock fillets**, skinned (sole, flounder, or orange roughy also work well)

2 T **Italian-style breadcrumbs**

1 tsp **olive oil**

- Preheat oven to 425 degrees.
- Coat an 8-by-11-inch (or similar size) baking dish with cooking spray and sprinkle bottom with lemon zest.
- *Make cheese sauce:* In a small bowl, whisk together ¼ cup of the milk and the flour until smooth. Heat remaining milk (1½ cups) in a heavy saucepan over medium heat until steaming. Add flour mixture to milk and cook, whisking constantly, until sauce bubbles and thickens, 2 to 3 minutes. Remove from heat. Stir in ½ cup Parmesan, black pepper to taste, and a pinch of cayenne.
- Meanwhile, cook spinach (See Spinach, page 9), drain and press out excess moisture. Spread spinach over bottom of prepared baking dish.
- Arrange fish fillets over spinach, overlapping slightly.
- Spoon cheese sauce evenly over fish and sprinkle with remaining 2 tablespoons Parmesan.
- In a small bowl, mix breadcrumbs and oil. Sprinkle over cheese sauce.
- Bake 30 to 35 minutes until golden and bubbly. Fish should flake when poked with a small, sharp knife.

Serves 4. Each serving supplies:
Calories(kcal) 290 Protein 34(g) Carbohydrates 25(g) Dietary Fiber 6(g) Cholesterol 81(mg) Fat 7(g) Sodium 554(mg)

Chicken Breasts Stuffed with Spinach and Mushrooms

Under cool, cloudy conditions, spinach grows like a weed — so a Central New York spring is its perfect accomplice. When spinach is fresh from the field, it's about five times as nutritious (and delicious), so I try to slip it into every meal.

Stuffing

1 tsp **olive oil**

½ cup finely chopped **onion**

1 **clove garlic**, minced

1 cup chopped **mushrooms**

3 cups **fresh baby spinach**, washed, dried, and coarsely chopped

⅛ tsp **salt**

⅛ tsp **freshly ground pepper**

Chicken

2 **egg whites**

2 tsp **Dijon mustard**

1 cup **panko breadcrumbs** (Japanese-style)

4 (4-5oz) **skinless, boneless chicken breast halves**, trimmed

Olive oil cooking spray

> This recipe lends itself well to my step-by-step style of cooking. I'll take 15 minutes in the morning to make the stuffing, then an additional 10 minutes late in the afternoon to slit, fill, and coat the chicken breasts. The final step is simply slipping them into the oven.

Preheat oven to 400 degrees.

To make stuffing:

- Heat oil in medium-size nonstick skillet over medium heat. Add onions and cook, stirring often, until softened and light golden, 3 to 4 minutes. Add garlic and mushrooms, increase heat to medium high, and cook 3 to 4 minutes. Add spinach and cook, stirring, until wilted, about 20 to 30 seconds. Remove from heat.
- Stir in salt and pepper and set aside to cool.

To prepare chicken:

- In a medium bowl, whisk egg whites and mustard.
- Pour breadcrumbs into a shallow bowl or pie plate.
- Place chicken breasts on a cutting board. Using a small, sharp knife, create a pocket by making a 3-inch horizontal slit along one side of each chicken breast half.
- Fill each pocket with one-quarter of the stuffing. Close breasts over stuffing and secure with toothpicks.
- Dip each piece of chicken in egg-white mixture, then roll in panko breadcrumbs.
- Spray a rimmed cooking sheet with olive oil spray. Arrange chicken on sheet and spray lightly with olive oil.
- Bake chicken for 30-35 minutes, switch oven to broil and broil chicken until top is golden, 30-60 seconds.

Serves 4. Each serving supplies:
Calories(kcal) 289 Protein 34(g) Carbohydrates 24(g) Dietary Fiber 1(g) Cholesterol 74(mg) Fat 5(g) Sodium 322(mg)

Linda's After-Dinner Salad

Every night for dinner, I serve a green salad. It's the ultimate example of my simple, fresh, and healthy approach to cooking. I usually keep it basic – lettuce, olive oil, vinegar, salt, and pepper. And while the salad goes on the table at the start of the meal, we eat it at the end – a leisurely habit I inherited from my Italian family.

I'm kind of a purist, so I tend to let the lettuce star in my everyday salad. I'm personally partial to romaine (and not a big fan of iceberg lettuce). In winter, I might choose a mixture of tender baby lettuce leaves. Whatever the season, feel free to add a little flourish of whatever is fresh and tasty, like grape tomatoes or cucumber cubes. Just don't let the extras overwhelm the lovely lettuce.

4 cups romaine lettuce leaves, washed and spun dry

1 T olive oil

Salt and pepper to taste

2 tsp white balsamic vinegar

- Place lettuce in salad bowl and sprinkle with olive oil and salt to taste (I use about ¼ teaspoon salt). Toss well, using tongs.
- Add vinegar and pepper. Toss again to coat leaves thoroughly.
- Taste and re-season if necessary.

Serves 4. Each serving supplies:
Calories(kcal) 41 Protein 1(g) Carbohydrates 2(g) Dietary Fiber 1(g) Cholesterol 0(mg) Fat 3(g) Sodium 5(mg)

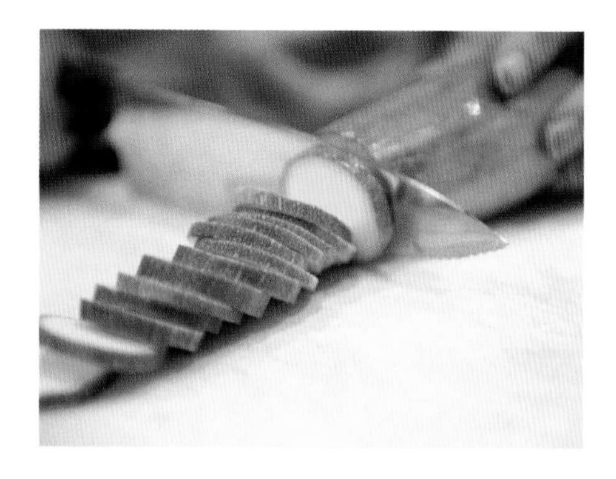

Hafner Zucchini and Cheese

This is my family's version of macaroni and cheese. It's fuss-free comfort food, without the guilt (or lethargy) that can follow an overdose of macaroni.

1 T olive oil

1 medium onion, thinly sliced

1 pound zucchini, sliced into ¼-inch rounds

½ cup fontina cheese, shredded

Salt and pepper to taste

- Place a large skillet over medium heat and add oil.
- Add onion and sauté until soft and translucent, about 3-4 minutes.
- Add zucchini slices and cook, stirring frequently, until soft and lightly browned. Season to taste.
- Turn off the heat and sprinkle with cheese (which will melt irresistibly into the nooks and crannies of the soft zucchini).
- Serve warm.

Serves 4. Each serving supplies:
Calories(kcal) 111 Protein 5(g) Carbohydrates 6(g) Dietary Fiber 2(g) Cholesterol 16(mg) Fat 8(g) Sodium 120(mg)

Sugar Snap Peas with Fresh Mint

One of my favorite rites of spring is serving the first snap peas – or the first anything – of the season!

6 cups sugar snap peas

1 T olive oil

1 T butter

Salt and pepper to taste

2 T chopped fresh mint leaves

- Bring about 5 quarts of water to a boil.
- Cook peas 2-3 minutes – they will turn bright green.
- Drain peas and return to pan. Stir in olive oil and butter. Season with salt and pepper. Sprinkle with mint and serve.

Serves 4. Each serving supplies:
Calories(kcal) 64 Protein 2(g) Carbohydrates 5(g) Dietary Fiber 2(g) Cholesterol 5(mg) Fat 4(g) Sodium 16(mg)

Zucchini Muffins

My parents (like many passionate gardeners) always have a bumper crop of zucchini. This is my mother's classic zucchini muffin recipe with my signature touch – substituting applesauce for some of the oil. Only your heart will know the difference!

2 cups **flour**

2 tsp **baking soda**

¼ tsp **baking powder**

1 tsp **salt**

3 tsp **cinnamon**

3 **eggs**

¼ cup **vegetable oil**

¾ cup **applesauce**

1½ cups **sugar**

2 tsp **vanilla extract**

1 tsp **lemon extract**

2 cups grated **zucchini**

1 cup **raisins**

1 cup **walnuts**

- Preheat oven to 350 degrees.
- Combine flour, baking soda, baking powder, salt, and cinnamon in a bowl.
- Combine eggs, oil, applesauce, sugar, vanilla, and lemon in a large bowl.
- Add dry ingredients to the egg mixture and stir gently to combine.
- Stir in zucchini, then the raisins and walnuts.
- Pour into lined muffin tins (about ⅔ full).
- Bake for 20 minutes or until toothpick inserted in muffin comes out clean.

Makes 24 muffins. Each muffin supplies:
Calories(kcal) 173 Protein 3(g) Carbohydrates 28(g) Dietary Fiber 1(g) Cholesterol 26(mg) Fat 6(g) Sodium 218(mg)

Fresh Strawberry Pie

In North Syracuse, for the better part of the last century, the name Hafner was synonymous with the best local strawberries. This pie is part of that family tradition.

1 **9-inch pie shell**, baked and cooled (See page 32, or use your favorite recipe)

1 cup **sugar**

3 T **cornstarch**

1 cup crushed **strawberries**

¼ cup **water**

1 T **lemon juice**

5 cups **fresh strawberries**, washed, hulled, and sliced

4 ounces **heavy cream**, chilled

1 T **powdered sugar**

½ tsp **vanilla extract**

- Combine the sugar, cornstarch, crushed strawberries, water, and lemon juice in a heavy-bottomed saucepan. Cook over medium heat, stirring, until mixture thickens — about 5 minutes. Set aside to cool.
- Combine the cooked mixture with the sliced strawberries.
- Pour into the pie shell and refrigerate until serving, at least 4 hours.
- When ready to serve, whip heavy cream with powdered sugar and vanilla.
- Spread whipped cream on top of pie and garnish with fresh strawberries.

Makes 1 pie, 9 inches in diameter (10 slices)

Serves 10. Each serving supplies:
Calories(kcal) 391 Protein 4(g) Carbohydrates 51(g) Dietary Fiber 3(g) Cholesterol 16(mg) Fat 20(g) Sodium 126(mg)

[You can easily use this recipe to make peach pie by simply substituting fresh peaches for the strawberries. If you use fresh peach slices as a garnish, dip them in lemon juice to keep them from turning brown.]

Strawberry-Rhubarb Pie

Chuck and I are so partial to this pie that my mother makes us each one for our birthdays. Since local rhubarb is often ripe before local strawberries, it's OK to jump the gun and make this with strawberries from Florida or California.

1 **(9-inch) double-pie crust** (See page 32, or use your favorite recipe)

2 cups sliced **strawberries**

2 cups sliced **rhubarb** (1-inch cubes)

¼ cup **tapioca**

1¼ cup **sugar**

1 T **butter**

- Preheat oven to 400 degrees.
- Mix strawberries, rhubarb, tapioca, and sugar and let stand for 15 minutes. Fill crust with fruit mixture and dot with butter.
- Cover with top crust and crimp edges to seal. Cut several slits in the crust.
- Bake for 45-50 minutes, or until juices bubble.
- Serve warm or at room temperature.

Makes 1 pie, 9 inches in diameter (10 slices).

Serves 10. Each serving supplies:
Calories(kcal) 362 Protein 3(g) Carbohydrates 51(g) Dietary Fiber 2(g) Cholesterol 3(mg) Fat 16(g) Sodium 129(mg)

Rhubarb Crumble

Crisps and crumbles are so easy to make. Much easier and healthier than a pie!

Rhubarb Filling

2 pounds **fresh rhubarb** cut into ½-inch pieces (or two 1-pound packages, frozen)

1¾ cups **sugar**

1 T **cornstarch**

1½ tsp **vanilla extract**

Topping

⅔ cup **oatmeal** (not instant)

⅓ cup **brown sugar**

⅓ cup **pecan** or walnut halves

2 T **canola oil**

- Preheat oven to 400 degrees.
- Coat a 13-by-9-inch baking dish with cooking spray.
- Toss all rhubarb filling ingredients together and allow fruit to macerate for about 15 minutes.
- Place all topping ingredients into the bowl of a food processor. Process until mixture just holds together.
- Spoon rhubarb mixture into the baking dish. Cover with topping mixture.
- Bake 35-40 minutes until top is browned and mixture is bubbling.

Serves 12. Each serving supplies:
Calories(kcal) 209 Protein 1(g) Carbohydrates 42(g) Dietary Fiber 2(g) Cholesterol 0(mg) Fat 5(g) Sodium 4(mg)

For Apple Crumble, simply replace the rhubarb with 8 medium apples, peeled, cored, and sliced. Reduce sugar to ½ cup, and omit the cornstarch and vanilla.

Sublime Strawberry Trifle

For very special occasions, I like to serve this spectacular swirl of strawberries, angel food cake, and cream (three varieties, no less!). It's not exactly for dieters, but I've managed, as usual, to lower the calorie count without sacrificing a morsel of flavor.

16 ounces **light cream cheese** (2 packages at room temperature)

1½ cups **powdered sugar**

1 cup **light sour cream**

3 tsp **vanilla extract**, divided

¼ tsp **almond extract**

1 cup **heavy cream**

1 9-inch **angel food cake** (see recipe, Page 31),
cut into 1½ inch cubes

2 quarts **fresh strawberries,** washed and thickly sliced

3-4 T **sugar**

Whole strawberries for garnish

- Using an electric mixer and a large bowl, combine cream cheese and powdered sugar. Blend in the sour cream, 2 teaspoons of the vanilla extract, and the almond extract.
- In a small bowl, whip the heavy cream and the remaining 1 teaspoon of vanilla until stiff. Fold into the cream cheese mixture. Fold in the angel food cake and mix well to coat cubes.
- In a separate bowl, combine the sliced strawberries and sugar to taste.
- In the bottom of a large glass (trifle) bowl, arrange about one-third of the sliced strawberries. Cover with one-half of the cream cheese/cake mixture. Repeat these two layers, then top with the remaining strawberries.
- Cover the bowl with plastic wrap and chill well before serving.
- Garnish, if desired, with whole strawberries.

Serves 12. Each serving supplies:
Calories (kcal) 429 Protein 10(g) Carbohydrates 64(g) Dietary Fiber 2(g) Cholesterol 52(mg) Fat 15(g) Sodium 306(mg)

Angel Food Cake

1 cup flour

1¼ cups powdered sugar

12 egg whites (about 1½ cups)

1½ tsp cream of tartar

¼ tsp salt

¾ cup granulated sugar

1½ tsp vanilla extract

½ tsp almond extract

- Preheat oven to 375 degrees.
- In a small bowl, combine the flour and powdered sugar and set aside.
- Place the egg whites, cream of tartar, and salt in a large bowl. With an electric mixer, beat at medium speed until foamy.
- Increase mixer speed to high and add the granulated sugar in increments, 2 tablespoons at a time. Once all the sugar is absorbed, continue to beat on high speed until stiff peaks form.
- Using a spatula, gently fold in the vanilla and almond extracts.
- Sprinkle the flour mixture — ¼ cup at a time — over the egg-white mixture. Using a spatula (or the mixer on low speed), gently fold in the flour until absorbed. Repeat with the remaining flour mixture, folding in ¼ cup at a time. Be careful not to overmix, or the egg whites will deflate.
- With a thin, rubber spatula, scrape the batter into an UNGREASED tube pan. To prevent air pockets from forming, gently cut through the poured batter with a knife.
- Bake the cake for 30 to 35 minutes or until the top springs back when touched with a finger.
- Remove from oven. Invert and place the open hole of the tube pan over a long-necked bottle. Cool completely.

Serves 12. Each serving supplies:
Calories(kcal) 154 Protein 5(g) Carbohydrates 34(g) Dietary Fiber 0(g) Cholesterol 0(mg) Fat 0(g) Sodium 105(mg)

It's easiest to separate egg whites when they're still cold from the refrigerator. But for maximum volume, let the egg whites come to room temperature before beating.

Pie Crust

Makes a 9-inch double-crust pie

2 cups flour

½ tsp salt

¾ cup butter-flavored shortening

¼ cup water, ice cold

- Mix the flour and salt in a medium bowl. Add the shortening. Using a pastry blender or two knives, cut the shortening into the flour until mixture forms pea-sized pieces.
- Sprinkle 2 tablespoons of the water over the mixture. Toss with a fork until moistened. Add the remaining water and stir until the dough holds together.
- Scoop the dough into a ball. Flatten it into a disc and wrap in plastic wrap. Chill.
- To roll out the crust, lightly dust a large cutting board with flour. Place the disc on the cutting board and dust it with flour. With a rolling pin, roll the dough into a circle, about 1/8-inch thick.
- Using a 9-inch pie plate as a guide, lightly trace a circle into the rolled dough. The circle should be about 2 inches wider than the outer rim of the pie plate. With the tip of a small, sharp knife, cut out the circle.
- Carefully fold the circle into halves, then quarters, and transfer to the pie plate. Unfold the dough and gently press into the bottom and sides of the pie plate. Fold the extra dough under at the edge of the plate. With a fork or your fingers, press – or crimp – the folded edge of the dough.
- To pre-bake an empty crust, preheat the oven to 450 degrees. Prick the crust with a fork on all sides.
- Bake for 12 minutes or until golden.
- Remove and completely cool the crust before filling.

Serves 10. Each serving supplies:
Calories(kcal) 223 Protein 3(g) Carbohydrates 19(g) Dietary Fiber 1(g) Cholesterol 0(mg) Fat 15(g) Sodium 119(mg)

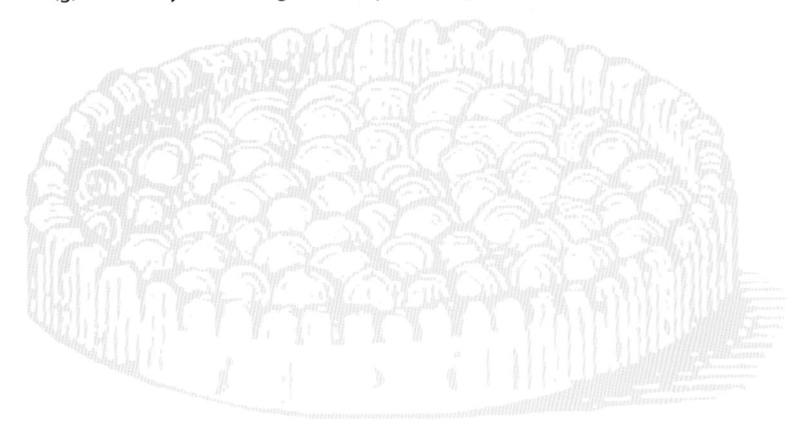

Summer: The Vibrant Season

Summer brings an embarrassment of riches to Central New York. A patchwork of glorious greens carpets our rolling hills. Our deep blue lakes sparkle like sapphires. Farmers' fields grow more vibrant by the hour. And those fragile greenhouse flowers we so recently nudged toward bloom? They've burst into bouquets of bold color — and now adorn decks, patios, porches, lawns, and gardens, far and wide.

As enchanting as I find our summer scenery, my heart skips a beat when the season's ultimate bounty — a rainbow of fresh, ripe produce — arrives daily at Chuck Hafner's. (I know it's been years since we outgrew our original farm stand, but that face-to-face, fresh-from-the-field model remains at the heart of our family business.)

Every summer, I am shocked once again by the superiority of our locally grown fruits and vegetables. Whether I'm biting into the season's first snap peas, cucumbers, corn, carrots, tomatoes, peaches, or melons, I can't wait to turn these treasures into meals and celebrations that will keep my family healthy, strong, and happy.

Summer

Corn

Chuck Hafner's sweet corn has been a treasured local commodity for more than 40 years. The corn sold at our garden center is picked fresh daily (twice a day in peak season). Field-to-table time is a critical factor when you're committed to selling – and serving – sweet, tender corn. Pedigree is also important: Super Sweet varieties of Butter and Sugar are our most popular.

Fresh, Simple, Healthy Recipe

Fresh Sweet Corn

To cook fresh corn:

- To keep the corn fresh, remove the husk as close as possible to serving time.
- When ready to serve, bring a large pot of water to a boil.
- Drop the ears of corn into boiling water and boil for 5 minutes.
- For maximum flavor, drain the corn and serve immediately.

One ear of corn:
Calories(kcal) 77 Protein 3(g) Carbohydrates 17(g) Dietary Fiber 2 (g) Cholesterol 0(mg) Fat 1(g) Sodium 14(mg)

[I know it's traditional to serve fresh corn with butter and salt. Believe it or not, it's just as delicious and kinder to your arteries unadorned, especially the new sweet varieties.)]

Fresh Lemonade from Scratch

If you want to surprise — and delight — your family or friends, serve this refreshing, old-fashioned drink. Yes, it's made "from scratch," but it couldn't be easier — a 10-minute undertaking, max! Best of all, you avoid all the unrecognizable ingredients in processed or powdered lemonade.

4 **lemons**

1 cup **sugar**

2 cups **water**

½ cup **fresh mint leaves**, washed

Additional **mint sprigs** and **lemon slices**, for garnish

- Prepare a "simple syrup" by pouring the water into a small saucepan. Stir in the sugar and place over medium heat, stirring until dissolved.
- Wash the lemons. Before juicing, press the heel of your hand into the lemons and roll them on the countertop to help release juice. Halve and squeeze the juice from the lemons. You should have about 1 cup of lemon juice.
- Combine the lemon juice with the simple syrup and transfer to a pitcher.
- Add 2 quarts of water, stir in the mint leaves, and chill.
- Served chilled lemonade over ice cubes and garnish with additional mint sprigs and lemon slices, if desired.

Serves 8. Each serving supplies:
Calories(kcal) 106 Protein 0(g) Carbohydrates 28(g)
Dietary Fiber 0(g) Cholesterol 0(mg) Fat 0(g)
Sodium 13(mg)

Presto Pesto Sauce

In my book, there's no such thing as too much basil. With the press of a button, I can transform these fragrant green leaves into pesto, an addictive blend of five signature Italian ingredients. The most vibrant and versatile sauce on the planet, pesto can be spread on bruschetta, tossed with pasta, slipped into a sandwich, or drizzled over grilled fish or chicken.

2 cups **fresh basil leaves**, washed and dried

2 **cloves garlic**, peeled

½ cup **pine nuts**

½ cup grated **Parmesan cheese**

½ cup **olive oil**

- Place the first four ingredients in the bowl of a food processor and blend to combine. Continue to blend while adding the olive oil in a slow, steady stream.
- To store, refrigerate pesto in a sealed container. If the oil separates, stir to blend before serving.

Serves 16. Each serving supplies:
Calories(kcal) 101 Protein 2(g) Carbohydrates 1(g) Dietary Fiber 0(g) Cholesterol 2(mg) Fat 10(g) Sodium 39(mg)

[Since pesto is a breeze to freeze, I use it year-round to deliver the essence of summer — on demand.]

Simple Salsa

There's a world of difference between fresh and supermarket salsa. See for yourself. It's actually relaxing to focus on chopping for a few minutes.

3 or 4 medium fresh tomatoes, chopped

1 small red, yellow, or green pepper, chopped

½ Vidalia (sweet) or red onion, chopped

1 jalapeno or Serrano chili, seeded, and chopped (optional)

¼ cup chopped cilantro

1-2 tsp fresh lime juice or white balsamic vinegar

Salt to taste

- Combine all ingredients in a bowl and allow to stand for 10 to 15 minutes, to mingle flavors.
- Salsa can be refrigerated for several hours before serving, but it tastes best when made the day it's served.

Serves 16 (1 Tablespoon each). Each serving supplies:
Calories(kcal) 11 Protein 0(g) Carbohydrates 2 (g) Dietary Fiber 0 (g) Cholesterol 0 (mg) Fat 0 (g) Sodium 6 (mg)

Fresh Peach Salsa

Salsa, like salad, is a creative opportunity. Feel free to improvise and make this sweet/tart salsa with your favorite fresh fruits. Plums, pineapple, and mango are other juicy options.

2 or 3 peaches or nectarines, peeled and chopped

1 small red bell pepper, chopped

1 T Vidalia (sweet) or red onion, chopped (or you can use green onions from your garden)

1 T chopped cilantro

1 to 2 tsp fresh lime juice

- Combine all ingredients in a bowl and allow to stand for 10 to 15 minutes, to mingle flavors.
- Salsa can be refrigerated for several hours before serving, but it tastes best when made the day it's served.
- Serve with grilled fish or chicken.

Serves 16 (1 Tablespoon each). Each serving supplies:
Calories(kcal) 8 Protein 0(g) Carbohydrates 2(g) Dietary Fiber 0(g) Cholesterol 0(mg) Fat 0(g) Sodium 0(mg)

Maria's Refrigerator Pickles

Home pickling is largely a lost art, but it's easy to revive if you take my cousin Maria's refrigerator approach, which provides overnight delivery of crunchy, tangy pickles in a memorable mustard hue.

6 cups thinly sliced, **unwaxed cucumbers** (unpeeled)

2 cups thinly sliced **sweet onions**, such as Vidalia

1 cup **sugar**

1½ cups **apple cider vinegar**

½ tsp **salt**

½ tsp **mustard seed**

½ tsp **celery seed**

½ tsp **ground turmeric**

- In a clean, 1-quart lidded jar, layer cucumbers and onions.
- In a small saucepan over medium-high heat, combine the remaining ingredients and bring to a boil.
- Immediately pour this mixture over the layered cucumbers and onions. Cool to room temperature, then cover the jar securely and refrigerate for at least 24 hours before serving.
- Pickles may be stored in the refrigerator for up to one month.

Makes 1 quart. Serves 48 (1 serving = 1/8 cup)
Calories(kcal) 22 Protein 0(g) Carbohydrates 5(g) Dietary Fiber 0(g) Cholesterol 0(mg) Fat 0(g) Sodium 26(mg)

Best-of-Show Gazpacho

When we visited my daughter Ryan during her semester in the Andalusia region of Spain, her host mother invited us to dinner and served this regional favorite – a chilled summer soup made with deep-flavored local tomatoes.

2 slices **day-old bread** (whole wheat or whole grain)

1 **red pepper**, seeded and chopped

1 **green pepper**, seeded and chopped

1 **cucumber**, seeded and chopped

1 pound **tomatoes**, peeled and chopped (preferably pear or Roma)

2 **cloves garlic**, peeled

2 **scallions**, sliced (white part only)

2 T **olive oil**

1 T **red wine vinegar**

1 T chopped **fresh parsley**

¼ tsp **salt**

- In a shallow bowl, soak the bread in water for 5 minutes, then squeeze the bread to extract the water.
- Place a little more than half of the red pepper, green pepper, and cucumber in the bowl of a food processor or blender, reserving the rest for garnish.
- Add the remaining ingredients (including the soaked bread) and process until smooth.
- Transfer the soup to a covered container and chill for at least 2 hours.
- To serve, ladle the soup into bowls and garnish with the reserved peppers and cucumber.

Serves 6. Each serving supplies:
Calories(kcal) 92 Protein 2(g) Carbohydrates 10(g) Dietary Fiber 3(g) Cholesterol 0(mg) Fat 5(g) Sodium 149 (mg)

[One note of caution:
Gazpacho gets its flavor from ripe, luscious, local tomatoes. You're taking a risk if you use anything but Central New York's finest!]

Chilled Green Beans with Mint

One of my greatest summer pleasures is stepping outside to my herb garden, where — with a few snips — I can give a familiar vegetable a fresh new spin.

1½ pounds **fresh green beans**

2 T **olive oil**

½ to 1 T **white balsamic vinegar**

2 **cloves garlic**, quartered

1 T chopped **fresh mint**

Salt and **pepper** to taste

- Trim and slice the beans into bite-size pieces. In a large saucepan, bring water to a boil. Add the green beans and cook for 3 to 4 minutes, until the beans are crisp-tender. Immediately drain the beans. Cool to room temperature, then store in the refrigerator until ready to serve.
- Just before serving, toss the beans with oil and vinegar. Toss again with the garlic and mint. Season with salt and pepper.

Serves 6. Each serving supplies:
Calories(kcal) 75 Protein 2(g) Carbohydrates 8(g) Dietary Fiber 3(g) Cholesterol 0(mg) Fat 5(g) Sodium 6(mg)

Tomato Salad Trio

When local tomatoes are in season, we rarely have a meal that doesn't feature these ripe, red beauties. Here are three simple tomato salads, each with a slightly different accent.

Tomato-Mozzarella Salad

4 **medium tomatoes**, sliced ¼-inch thick
8 ounces **fresh mozzarella**, sliced ¼-inch thick
2 T **olive oil**
¼ cup minced **fresh basil**
Salt and **pepper** to taste

- On a serving plate, alternate the tomato and mozzarella slices. Drizzle with the olive oil and sprinkle with basil. Season with salt and pepper. Serve at room temperature.

Serves 4-6. Each serving supplies:
Calories(kcal) 194 Protein 9(g) Carbohydrates 4(g) Dietary Fiber 1(g) Cholesterol 32(mg) Fat 15(g) Sodium 141(mg)

Simple Tomato Salad

4 **medium tomatoes**, in ¼-inch slices
2 T **olive oil**
1 T minced **fresh oregano**
½ tsp **dried oregano**
Salt and **pepper** to taste

- On a serving plate, arrange the tomato slices. Drizzle with olive oil and sprinkle with the fresh and dried oregano. Season with salt and pepper. Serve at room temperature.

Serves 4-6. Each serving supplies:
Calories(kcal) 67 Protein 1(g) Carbohydrates 4(g) Dietary Fiber 1(g) Cholesterol 0 (mg) Fat 6 (g) Sodium 5(mg)

Super-Simple Tomato Salad

4 **medium tomatoes**, cut into wedges
2 T **olive oil**
2 T minced **fresh parsley**
1-2 **cloves garlic**, halved (optional)
Salt and **pepper** to taste

- Place the tomato wedges in a serving bowl. Add the olive oil, parsley and garlic. Toss gently. Season with salt and pepper. Serve at room temperature.

Serves 4-6. Each serving supplies:
Calories(kcal) 66 Protein 1(g) Carbohydrates 4(g) Dietary Fiber 1(g) Cholesterol 0(mg) Fat 6(g) Sodium 6(mg)

Do not refrigerate tomatoes, they will lose their flavor.

Bonanza Bean Salad

Two-bean salads are familiar summer fare. This recipe adds grape tomatoes and artichoke hearts for a boost of flavor, texture, and color.

½ pound **fresh green beans**, trimmed and cut into 2-inch pieces

1 (15 oz) can **garbanzo**, **red kidney**, or **cannelini beans**

1 pint **grape tomatoes**, halved

1 (14 oz) can **artichoke hearts packed in water**, drained and chopped

¼ cup sliced **red** or Vidalia onion

¼ cup finely chopped **parsley**

Tarragon Dressing

¼ cup **white balsamic vinegar**

2 tsp **Dijon mustard**

1 tsp **honey** or maple syrup

1 **clove garlic**, peeled

¼ tsp **salt**

⅛ tsp **black pepper**

4 T **olive oil**

1 T chopped **fresh tarragon**

- In a medium saucepan, bring water to a boil. Add the green beans and cook for 3 to 4 minutes, until the beans are crisp-tender. Immediately drain the beans and cool.
- Make the dressing by combining the vinegar, mustard, honey, garlic, salt, and pepper in a blender or food processor until smooth. With machine running, gradually add the oil and tarragon.
- In a large serving bowl, toss the cooked green beans with the remaining salad ingredients.
- Pour the dressing over the salad and toss to coat. Serve at room temperature.

Serves 8. Each serving supplies:
Calories(kcal) 181 Protein 5(g) Carbohydrates 25(g) Dietary Fiber 5(g) Cholesterol 0(mg) Fat 8(g) Sodium 569(mg)

Classic Potato Salad

We don't think of potatoes as a summer vegetable, but I love the tender – not jumbo – potatoes harvested early in the season. They're perfect for this traditional picnic favorite.

8 medium potatoes

5 eggs, hard-boiled

¾ cup chopped celery (about 2 ribs)

¼ cup chopped Vidalia (sweet) or red onion

¼ cup chopped red bell pepper

1¼ cup light mayonnaise

Paprika, to garnish

Salt and pepper to taste

- Wash the unpeeled potatoes and place in a large pot. Cover with water, bring to a boil, and cook until tender when pierced with a fork. Drain and cool.
- Peel and dice the potatoes into ½-inch cubes. Peel and chop 4 of the hardboiled eggs, reserving the fifth egg to slice and garnish the salad.
- Place the diced potatoes and eggs in a large bowl and mix in the celery, onion, and bell pepper. Fold in the mayonnaise and season with salt and pepper. Garnish the salad with the sliced egg and a dusting of paprika.
- Refrigerate salad if not serving immediately.

Serves 8-10. Each serving supplies:
Calories(kcal) 250 Protein 7(g) Carbohydrates 27(g) Dietary Fiber 2(g) Cholesterol 129 (mg) Fat 14(g) Sodium 270(mg)

[I often cook the potatoes a day ahead and refrigerate until needed. Sometimes I make the entire salad ahead, adding everything except the mayonnaise and sliced-egg garnish.]

Italian "Salt" Potato Salad

Syracuse – the salt city – is the proud home of salt potatoes. I'm a big fan of these bite-size potatoes, but I'm not a fan of the salt used to cook them. My solution is to skip the salt bath and season the cooked potatoes Italian-style, with healthy olive oil and white balsamic vinegar.

2½ pounds **salt potatoes**

1 pound **green beans**

½ **red onion**, peeled and thinly sliced

1 (6-oz) can **sliced black olives**, drained

1 tsp **dried oregano**

¼ cup **fresh basil leaves**, chopped

¼ cup **olive oil**

2 T **white balsamic vinegar**

- Rinse and lightly scrub the potatoes to remove any surface dirt. Place the potatoes in a large pot, cover with water, bring to a boil and cook until tender when pierced with a fork, about 20 minutes.
- Drain and cool the potatoes. Peel, if desired, then halve and slice into bite-size pieces (about 6 pieces per potato).
- Meanwhile, trim the beans and slice into 2-inch pieces. In a saucepan, bring 2 quarts of water to a boil. Add the beans and cook until tender but still crisp, about 5 to 7 minutes. Drain and cool.
- In a serving bowl, toss the beans with potatoes. Add the onion, olives, oregano, and basil. Drizzle with the olive oil and season with salt and ground pepper. Add the vinegar and toss lightly.
- Serve at room temperature. May be stored in the refrigerator for up to 24 hours.

Serves 8-10. Each serving supplies:
Calories(kcal) 184 Protein 3(g) Carbohydrates 26(g) Dietary Fiber 4(g) Cholesterol 0(mg) Fat 8(g) Sodium 175 (mg)

[To maximize the flavor of this salad, I make it early in the day and refrigerate it, so the flavors have time to mingle and mellow. Taste before serving – you may need to add a little more oil or vinegar.]

Pictured next page

Better Broccoli Salad

This is my makeover of a popular salad that traditionally includes high-fat ingredients. By using turkey bacon and light mayonnaise, I've given the crunchy salad a cleaner bill of health, without sacrificing its signature sweet-and-sour flavor.

2 bunches **broccoli**

1 bunch **radishes**

8 slices **turkey bacon**

½ cup shredded **cheddar cheese**

2 T chopped **red onion**

Dressing

2 T **apple cider vinegar**

1 cup **light mayonnaise**

¼ cup **sugar**

- Cut broccoli into small florets; wash and drain. Wash and cut the radishes into thin slices.
- Cook the bacon until crisp (I use the microwave). Drain and crumble bacon.
- In a serving bowl, combine the broccoli florets, radishes, bacon, cheese, and onion.
- To make dressing, combine the vinegar, mayonnaise, and sugar in a small bowl.
- Toss the broccoli mixture with the dressing and chill for at least two hours, until ready to serve.

Serves 8-10. Each serving supplies:
Calories(kcal) 213 Protein 8(g) Carbohydrates 17(g) Dietary Fiber 4(g) Cholesterol 27(mg) Fat 14(g) Sodium 416(mg)

Salt Potato Salad and Better Broccoli Salad shown at left.

Cool Cucumber Salad

Simple, crunchy, cool, and delicious – what could be more refreshing on a hot summer day?

2 cucumbers

1 T extra virgin olive oil

2 tsp white balsamic vinegar

Salt and pepper to taste

Fresh or dried oregano to taste

- Peel the cucumbers and slice into discs, about ¼-inch thick.
- Place the cucumbers in a shallow bowl and drizzle with the olive oil. Toss, add the vinegar, and toss again. Season with salt and pepper, sprinkle with oregano, and serve.

Serves 4. Each serving supplies:
Calories(kcal) 56 Protein 1(g) Carbohydrates 6(g) Dietary Fiber 1(g) Cholesterol 0(mg) Fat 4(g) Sodium 3(mg)

In a salad this fresh and pure, extra-virgin olive oil adds a subtle layer of flavor.

Tortellini with Grape Tomatoes and Corn

When I bring a bowl of this salad to a pot-luck affair it's so popular there are never any leftovers and everyone asks for the recipe.

9 oz package **fresh cheese tortellini**, uncooked

3 ears **fresh corn**, cooked 3 minutes (see Corn, Page 35), cut from the cob

1 clove **garlic**

2 cups **grape tomatoes**, sliced in half

¼ cup **green onion**, chopped

¼ cup **fresh basil**, chopped

1 tsp **olive oil**

⅛ tsp **pepper**

2 T Parmesan cheese

- Cook tortellini in boiling water 3 min. Add corn, cook 2-3 more minutes, drain well
- Rub the inside of a large serving bowl with garlic, discard garlic. Add tortellini, corn, tomatoes, and remaining ingredients. Toss gently to coat.

Serves 6. Each serving supplies:
Calories(kcal) 195 Protein 8 (g) Carbohydrates 31 (g) Dietary Fiber 2 (g) Cholesterol 19 (mg) Fat 5(g) Sodium 182(mg)

[When fresh sweet corn is out of season, frozen corn – especially organic – makes a fine substitute.]

Go Orange! Carrot Salad

I'm all for anything that helps kids eat healthy foods, so I've given this crisp summer salad a silly name and a few sweet surprises. Adults are also welcome to indulge!

¼ cup **raisins**

1 pound **carrots**, peeled

1 T **lemon juice**

1 T **orange juice**

¼ cup **low-fat sour cream**

¼ cup **light mayonnaise**

2 T **sugar**

½ tsp **salt**

⅓ cups **diced peaches**, plums, or fresh pineapple

- To plump the raisins, cover with boiling water for about 5 minutes, then drain.
- Grate the carrots by hand or in a food processor with a grating blade. Transfer the carrots to a bowl, add the lemon juice and orange juice, and toss.
- In a small bowl, whisk together the sour cream, mayonnaise, sugar, and salt. Toss with the carrots. Mix in the raisins and diced fruit, and serve.

Serves 4-6. Each serving supplies:
Calories(kcal) 143   Protein 2(g)   Carbohydrates 24(g)   Dietary Fiber 3(g)   Cholesterol 9(mg)   Fat 6(g)   Sodium 383(mg)

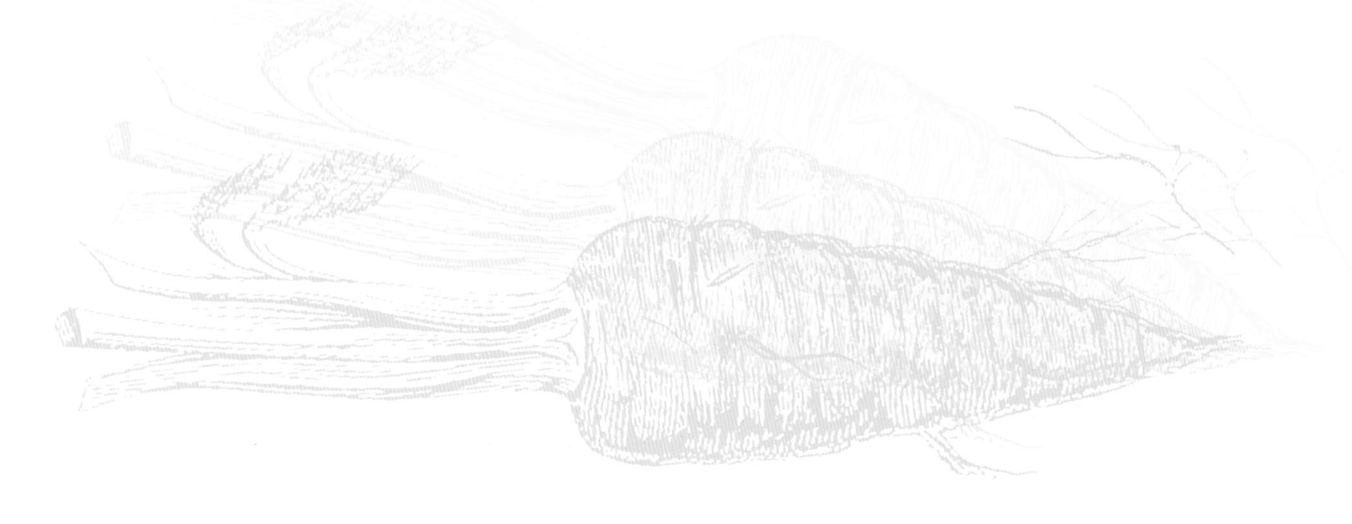

Pure Plum Tomato Sauce

If I had to choose one recipe to illustrate my cooking philosophy, this would be the one. It's utterly simple, fresh, and healthy. And it comes straight from Italy, by way of my great-uncle's daughter's husband, who happens to be a chef. Don't be alarmed by the nine cloves of garlic. They melt into the sauce and add amazing depth to the fresh, sweet tomatoes.

10 **fresh plum tomatoes** (or round)

¼ cup **olive oil**

9 **cloves garlic**, minced

1 tsp **salt**

⅛ tsp **ground black pepper**

1 tsp **sugar** (if necessary)

½ cup **fresh basil leaves**, chopped

grated **Romano cheese**, for garnish

- Halve the tomatoes, then cut into ½-inch cubes.
- Add the oil to a large skillet and toss in the garlic. Place over medium heat and stir — watching closely — until very lightly browned, about 1 minute.
- Add the tomatoes, salt, pepper, sugar, and basil to the saucepan. Cook for 15 minutes.
- Serve over angel-hair pasta, garnished with grated Romano cheese.

Serves 4-6. Each serving of sauce supplies:
Calories(kcal) 93 Protein 1(g) Carbohydrates 5(g) Dietary Fiber 1(g) Cholesterol 0(mg) Fat 8(g) Sodium 343(mg)

A sauce this pure and simple is all about the tomatoes — I reserve this recipe for when Central New York's plum tomatoes are at their peak.

United Nations Quesadillas

I love to mingle different cuisines, as in this fusion of classic Italian ingredients, wrapped in a Mexican tortilla and grilled American-style! It makes a great appetizer, lunch, or light dinner.

4 (8-inch) **flour tortillas**

12 oz grated or sliced **fresh mozzarella**

2 **tomatoes**, sliced ¼-inch thick

½ tsp **salt**

½ tsp **ground black pepper**

1 cup **fresh basil leaves**

- Preheat grill to medium heat.
- Place the tortillas on a cutting board. Arrange the tomatoes on one half of each tortilla. Top the tomatoes with the mozzarella and basil leaves.
- Season with salt and pepper.
- Place the quesadillas around the perimeter of the grill until the cheese melts and the tortillas are golden. Fold the tortilla in half over the fillings.
- Immediately cut the quesadillas into wedges and serve.

Serves 4. Each serving supplies:
Calories(kcal) 398 Protein 20(g) Carbohydrates 26(g) Dietary Fiber 2(g) Cholesterol 60(mg) Fat 22(g) Sodium 846(mg)

[Substitute rustic bread for the tortillas, and this becomes panini!]

Sage Turkey Burgers

These zesty, juicy patties prove that healthy can be irresistibly tasty!

1 pound **ground turkey breast**

1 **egg**

½ cup **dried breadcrumbs**

1 clove **garlic**, minced

¼ cup **onion**, finely chopped

1 T chopped **fresh sage**

1 tsp **poultry seasoning**

1 T **milk**

½ tsp **salt**

¼ tsp **pepper**

- In a large bowl, blend all ingredients. Form mixture into patties (4-6). Since the mixture is sticky, it's easier to work with if you wet your hands.
- Grill over medium heat, turning once. The burgers are done when they are no longer pink in the center.

Serves 4-6. Each serving supplies:
Calories(kcal) 201 Protein 19(g) Carbohydrates 10(g) Dietary Fiber 1(g) Cholesterol 114(mg) Fat 9(g) Sodium 417(mg)

[Garnish to your heart's delight — literally — by topping these healthy burgers with lettuce, tomato, onion, and guacamole — the works!]

[Fajitas are even more fun if you serve other Tex-Mex condiments such as guacamole, salsa, sour cream — the more the merrier.]

Tequila Fajitas

A make-your-own fajita bar is great for summer barbecues. This recipe is from my daughter, Ryan, and her husband, Ian. I love it when the next generation brings healthy options to the table!

Marinade

Juice of 3 **lemons**

1/8 cup **tequila**

1 tsp **red pepper flakes**

1 tsp **chili powder**

4 **garlic cloves**, crushed

Filling

1 pound **boneless chicken** or steak

1 **red bell pepper**

1 **yellow bell pepper**

1 **red onion**

Finish

4 **tortillas**, preferably whole wheat

1 cup shredded **Mexican cheese**

¼ cup chopped **fresh cilantro**

- In a shallow dish, combine the lemon juice, tequila, red pepper flakes, chili powder, and garlic. Add the chicken or steak and marinate in the refrigerator for 1 hour.
- Meanwhile, slice the peppers and onion into ½ -inch strips.
- To cook, grill the chicken or steak over medium-high heat.
- Place the peppers and onions in a grill pan sprayed with canola oil. Cook on the grill over medium-high heat, turning occasionally, until soft and lightly charred.
- Place the tortillas on the grill briefly to warm and slightly toast.
- To serve, slice the chicken or steak into 1-inch strips. Divide among the 4 tortillas, arranging the meat in a strip down the center. Top with the peppers and onions. Sprinkle with cheese and cilantro. Fold the tortilla sides to overlap in the center and serve.

Serves 4. Each serving supplies:
Calories(kcal) 446 Protein 36(g) Carbohydrates 35(g) Dietary Fiber 4(g) Cholesterol 98(mg) Fat 15(g) Sodium 505(mg) (Please note: Marinade is not included in the nutritional analysis.)

Guacamole

2 ripe **avocadoes**

1 T **red onion**, minced

1 clove **garlic**, minced

½ cup chopped **tomatoes**

1 T chopped **fresh cilantro**

2 tsp **fresh lime juice**

Salt and **pepper** to taste

- Peel and remove the pits from the avocadoes. Transfer to a small bowl and mash with a fork to desired consistency.
- Stir in the onion, garlic, tomatoes, cilantro, and lime juice. Season with salt and pepper.
- If not serving immediately, place an avocado pit in the guacamole and cover bowl securely with plastic wrap. Remove the pit before serving.

Serves 12 (2 Tablespoons each.) Each serving supplies:
Calories(kcal) 56 Protein 1(g) Carbohydrates 3(g) Dietary Fiber 2(g) Cholesterol 0(mg) Fat 5(g) Sodium 3(mg)

Red, White, and Green Piadine

Piadine is a chewy, grilled Italian flatbread that has been around for centuries and remains very popular in the Emilia Romagna region of Italy. It's terrific topped with sandwich fixings or salad greens. My version features some of each. If you don't have time to make your own piadine, store-bought Naan or flat bread will work just fine.

Piadine dough

- 1 package **active dry yeast**
- 1 cup **warm water**
- 3¾ cups **all-purpose flour**
- 2 T **olive oil**
- 1 tsp **salt**

Chicken, Spinach, and Red Pepper Filling

- 2¼ cups **roasted red peppers**
- 1 T minced **garlic**
- **Salt and pepper** to taste
- ⅓ cup grated **Parmesan cheese**
- 2 T finely chopped **fresh oregano** (or basil, if preferred)
- 9 cups loosely packed **spinach**
- 3 **cooked chicken breasts**, shredded or diced
- 1½ cups diced **fresh mozzarella**

Vinaigrette

- 3 T **orange juice** (preferably fresh)
- 1 T **white balsamic vinegar**
- ¼ cup **olive oil**
- **Salt** and **pepper** to taste

Serves 6. Each serving supplies:
Calories(kcal) 631 Protein 32(g) Carbohydrates 68(g) Dietary Fiber 4(g) Cholesterol 67(mg) Fat 24(g) Sodium 647(mg)

- In a large bowl, stir together the yeast, water, and about 2 tablespoons flour. Let stand until foamy (indicating that the yeast is working), about 10 minutes.
- With a wooden spoon, stir in 3 cups of flour, the oil, and salt. Or, use the dough hook attachment of your mixer. Turn onto a lightly floured surface and knead until smooth, about 5 minutes, adding more flour if necessary to make a soft dough.
- Shape the dough into a ball, cover it with a towel, and let rise until almost doubled in size, about 1 hour.
- Punch down the dough and knead for two more minutes. Divide into 6 equal pieces. (At this point, you may freeze the dough balls for up to 1 month. To use frozen dough, transfer to a bowl and defrost and let rise in the refrigerator.)
- On a lightly floured surface, roll each piece of dough into a circle about ¼-inch thick and 6-8 inches in diameter.
- Preheat the grill or griddle to high. Prick the dough with a fork. Lower the heat to medium and cook the piadine on the grill until golden, about 2-3 minutes per side. Repeat with remaining dough balls.
- In the bowl of a food processor, combine the roasted peppers and garlic. Blend until smooth. Season with salt and pepper.
- Spread 3 tablespoons of the pepper puree on each piadine. Sprinkle with 1 tablespoon of Parmesan cheese and 1 teaspoon oregano.
- In the bottom of a large bowl, whisk together the vinaigrette ingredients. Add the spinach, chicken, and mozzarella to the bowl, and toss with the vinaigrette. Divide this "salad" among the piadines, and serve folded in half (or open-faced, if preferred.)

Grilled Bourbon-Soy Salmon with Peach Salsa

4 (6-oz) **salmon fillets**

Marinade

¼ cup **brown sugar**

¼ cup **bourbon**

2 T **lower-sodium soy sauce**

1 T **fresh lime juice**

1 tsp **fresh ginger**, grated

¼ tsp **ground black pepper**

2 **garlic cloves**, crushed

Peach Salsa, page 41

- Combine the marinade ingredients in a large plastic bag with a sealable top.
- Add the salmon, seal the bag, and marinate in the refrigerator for 30 minutes, turning the bag once.
- Remove the salmon from the bag and discard marinade.
- Preheat grill to medium-high heat. Grill the salmon for 5 minutes on each side, or until it flakes when a fork is inserted.
- Serve salmon with Peach Salsa.

Serves 4. Each serving supplies:
Calories(kcal) 215 Protein 37(g) Carbohydrates 0(g) Dietary Fiber 0(g) Cholesterol 97(mg) Fat 6(g) Sodium 124(mg). (Please note: Marinade is not included in the nutritional analysis.)

Perfect Peach Shortcake

When local peaches are bursting with flavor, my first instinct is to celebrate with an old-fashioned shortcake. This recipe is also perfect with fresh strawberries.

Biscuits

- 2 cups **all-purpose flour**
- 2 T **sugar**
- 3 tsp **baking powder**
- ½ tsp **salt**
- ½ cup **Smart Balance** or cold butter
- 1 **egg**, slightly beaten
- ⅔ cup 1% **milk**

Filling

- 6-8 **fresh peaches**
- 1 T **lemon juice**
- ¼ cup **sugar** or less if fruit is extra sweet

Topping

Whipped cream or plain yogurt sweetened to taste with honey and cinnamon

- Preheat oven to 425 degrees.
- In a mixing bowl, stir together the flour, sugar, baking powder, and salt. Add the Smart Balance or butter and work into the flour with a pastry blender, until the mixture looks like coarse crumbs. (Two knives also work; just cross them in the bowl and pull in opposite directions.)
- Stir in the egg and milk just until blended. To keep the dough tender, do not overmix.
- With a large spoon, drop the dough into 8 mounds, about 2 inches apart, onto an ungreased cookie sheet.
- Bake the biscuits for about 12 minutes or until light golden brown.
- Makes 8 biscuits

To assemble

- Peel, pit, and slice the peaches. Toss in a bowl and add the lemon juice (to keep the peaches from turning brown). Add sugar to taste (I use approximately ¼ cup for ripe, local peaches.)
- Cut the biscuits in half and layer with the sliced peaches.
- Top each with one tablespoon of whipped cream or yogurt.

(If you don't use all the biscuits, freeze them — or serve them the next morning with homemade jam.)

Serves 16. Each serving supplies:
Calories(kcal) 142 Protein 3(g) Carbohydrates 22(g) Dietary Fiber 1(g) Cholesterol 14(mg) Fat 5(g) Sodium 220(mg)

Fruit Pizza

This glorious dessert is easy to deliver if tackled in increments. I usually make the "pizza" crust the night before — or freeze it one week ahead — and the cream-cheese filling the morning before it's served. Then comes the fun: arranging and glazing the beautiful summer fruit!

Sugar Cookie Crust

1 cup **softened butter**, or Smart Balance

¾ cup **powdered sugar**

⅓ cup **sugar**

1 **egg**

½ tsp **vanilla extract**

¼ tsp **almond extract** (optional)

2½ cups **flour**

2½ tsp **baking soda**

2½ tsp **cream of tartar**

Filling

16 ounces **light cream cheese**, at room temperature

¾ cup **powdered sugar**

1 tsp **vanilla extract**

Fruit Topping

4 **peaches**, peeled and sliced

1 quart **strawberries**, hulled and sliced

1 pint **blueberries**

Use your imagination. You can use any fresh fruit in any combination: grapes, kiwi, plums, or berries work well.

Orange Sauce

½ cup **sugar**

1 cup **orange juice**

¼ cup fresh **lemon juice**

4 tsp **cornstarch**

¼ tsp grated **orange peel**

¼ tsp grated **lemon peel**

- Preheat the oven to 325 degrees.
- In a large bowl, cream the butter and sugars until light and fluffy. Add the egg, vanilla, and almond extract and beat well.
- Combine the dry ingredients and gradually add to the creamed mixture, blending well.
- Divide the dough into two pieces. With lightly floured hands, pat into two lightly greased pizza pans, 12 inches in diameter. Bake for 12 to 15 minutes, until lightly colored. Remove from oven and cool.
- With an electric mixer, whip together the cream cheese, powdered sugar, and vanilla. Spread mixture over cooled crusts. Arrange the fruit slices on top.
- In a small saucepan, combine the sugar, orange, and lemon juices, and cornstarch. Cook over medium heat, stirring constantly, until sauce thickens. Stir in the orange and lemon peels. Cool the sauce to room temperature. When cool, use a pastry brush or spoon to glaze the fruit with the sauce.
- Chill tart until ready to serve. Serve the fruit pizza the day it's made or the crust will become soggy.

Makes 2 Pizzas. Serves 18. Each serving supplies:

Calories(kcal) 325 Protein 5(g) Carbohydrates 45(g) Dietary Fiber 2(g) Cholesterol 51(mg) Fat 15(g) Sodium 371(mg)

On-the-Go Oatmeal Parfait

When we have a day of hiking or river rafting ahead, I make a batch of this cold peach-berry oatmeal the night before. A variation of the Swiss breakfast food known as muesli, it's tasty and hearty but not heavy – the perfect portable breakfast.

2 cups **oatmeal**, uncooked (not instant)

8-ounce carton **plain low-fat yogurt** (if you prefer it sweeter use low-fat vanilla yogurt)

2 cups sliced **fresh peaches** and **blueberries**

1½ cups **apple juice**

1 tsp **vanilla extract**

- In a bowl, combine oatmeal, yogurt, fruit, apple juice, and vanilla.
- Cover and refrigerate 8 hours or overnight.
  May be stored in the refrigerator for up to 4 days before serving.

Serves 4-6. Each serving supplies:
Calories(kcal) 212 Protein 7(g) Carbohydrates 41(g) Dietary Fiber 5(g) Cholesterol 3(mg) Fat 3(g) Sodium 28(mg)

Autumn: The Golden Season

'o lure us away from summer's pleasures, nature plays a lever hand, bewitching us with blazing leaves, flickering umpkins, and juicy apples by the bushel. I for one, find utumn irresistible. This is officially harvest season. Fall's ull-strength crops — fiery orange squash, dark leafy greens, uby red apples — are dense with flavor, not to mention utrition. Did you know that the healthiest foods are those vith the deepest colors?

As soon as the shadows start to lengthen (and the days tart to shorten), I feel the call of the kitchen. Things are still uzzing at the garden center. Last season alone, we sold more han 20,000 pumpkins from the Hafner pumpkin farm. But nce the autumn sun goes down, you'll find me snug in my itchen, peeling, roasting, simmering, baking — and making he most of this gorgeous season.

Fall

Roasted Eggplant Dip

Despite its regal purple robe, the eggplant is quite a chameleon. It quietly carries more assertive flavors — like the sesame taste of tahini — yet retains its own distinct texture. I warn you, this dip is addictive. But with raw veggies or low-fat chips, it's a guilt-free indulgence.

2 large eggplants

1 T fresh lemon juice

2 T tahini (sesame seed paste)

2 cloves garlic, finely minced

Salt and pepper to taste

2 T finely chopped Italian parsley

- Preheat oven to 400 degrees. Spray or brush baking sheet with canola oil.
- Halve the eggplants and place cut-side down on the baking sheet. Roast for about 40 minutes or until pulp pierces easily with a fork. Remove from oven and allow to cool.
- With a large spoon, scoop out the pulp, discarding the seeds and skin.
- Transfer pulp to food processor. Add lemon juice, tahini, and garlic. Process until smooth.
- Season with salt and pepper, spoon into a serving bowl, and garnish with parsley.
- Serve with raw vegetables or low-fat chips.

Serves 24 (1 Tablespoon each). Each serving supplies:
Calories(kcal) 17 Protein 1(g) Carbohydrates 3(g) Dietary Fiber 1(g) Cholesterol 0(mg) Fat 1(g) Sodium 1(mg)

[This healthy dip also makes a tasty sandwich spread — and a great alternative to mayonnaise.]

Cauliflower Frittata Muffins

2 T olive oil

2 cups minced Vidalia (sweet) onion

1 T minced garlic

5 cups cauliflower chopped in ½- inch pieces

1 cup chopped bell pepper, red, orange, or yellow

¼ cup unseasoned breadcrumbs

3 T minced fresh basil

10 large eggs

3 T minced fresh parsley

1 cup crumbled feta or goat cheese

Salt and pepper to taste

- Preheat oven to 350 degrees. Use cooking spray to grease the bottoms and sides of 12 muffin tins.
- Pour the oil into a large lidded frying pan and place over medium heat. Add the onion and sauté until soft, about 4 minutes.
- Add the garlic, cauliflower, and bell peppers. Cover and cook until tender, about 6 minutes. Remove from heat.
- Add the breadcrumbs and basil and stir to combine.
- Crack the eggs into a bowl and whisk until smooth. Stir in the parsley and cheese and add to the cauliflower mixture.
- Divide the egg mixture evenly among the muffin tins and bake until firm, 25 to 30 minutes.

Serves 12. Each serving supplies:
Calories(kcal) 145 Protein 8(g) Carbohydrates 7(g) Dietary Fiber 2(g) Cholesterol 187(mg) Fat 9(g) Sodium 220(mg)

Roasted Fall Vegetables

I'm delighted to see that roasting vegetables is catching on like wildfire. What's not to love? This ancient cooking method concentrates the vegetables' sweetness and creates a delicious bronze crust.

1 parsnip

2 carrots

1 sweet potato (good-sized)

1 sweet onion (large)

2 cups broccoli florets

1 red or yellow sweet pepper

2 T olive oil

Salt and freshly ground pepper to taste

- Preheat oven to 400 degrees.
- Peel and/or cut vegetables into bite-size cubes. Combine in mixing bowl and toss with olive oil. Season with salt and pepper.
- Transfer vegetables to roasting pan and roast for 25 minutes, turning vegetables about halfway through.

Serves 4-6. Each serving supplies:
Calories(kcal) 151 Protein 3(g) Carbohydrates 24(g) Dietary Fiber 5(g) Cholesterol 0(mg) Fat 6(g) Sodium 50(mg)

[**Feel free to personalize this dish with your favorite vegetables and herbs, such as fresh beets, butternut squash or a sprig of rosemary. The more the merrier!**]

Maple-Roasted Sweet Potatoes

Almost too good to be good for you! You don't need much maple syrup, but you should definitely use the real thing.

3 large sweet potatoes

2 T olive oil

2 T pure maple syrup

Salt and freshly ground black pepper to taste

fresh parsley for garnish (optional)

- Preheat oven to 350 degrees.
- Peel sweet potatoes and cut into 1-inch cubes.
- In a mixing bowl, toss the sweet potatoes with oil and maple syrup.
- Season with salt and pepper.
- Transfer to a shallow baking dish and roast for 45 minutes or until tender when pierced with fork. About halfway through, turn with a spatula so potatoes brown evenly. Sprinkle with parsley if desired.

Serves 4-6. Each serving supplies:
Calories(kcal) 166 Protein 2(g) Carbohydrates 28(g) Dietary Fiber 4(g) Cholesterol 0(mg) Fat 6(g) Sodium 40(mg)

Sweet Potato Casserole

2½ pounds sweet potatoes, scrubbed

2 large eggs, lightly beaten

2 T unsalted butter, melted, plus a bit more for preparing the pan

2 T pure maple syrup

1 tsp salt

½ tsp ground cinnamon

½ tsp ground ginger

Freshly ground black pepper to taste

¼ cup coarsely chopped pecans

- Preheat oven to 400 degrees.
- Pierce each sweet potato 2-3 times with a fork and place on baking sheet. Bake for 45 to 50 minutes, until tender, and set aside to cool. Reduce oven temperature to 350 degrees.
- Scoop pulp from cooled sweet potatoes, discarding skins. Transfer potatoes into a medium bowl and mash until smooth.
- Add eggs, melted butter, maple syrup, salt, cinnamon, ginger, and pepper. Whisk mixture until blended.
- Lightly grease an 8-by-8-inch ovenproof dish with butter. Spread sweet potato mixture into dish and sprinkle the top with pecans.
- Bake until puffed, about 30 minutes. Serve immediately.

Serves 6-8. Each serving supplies:
Calories(kcal) 238 Protein 5(g) Carbohydrates 38(g) Dietary Fiber 6(g) Cholesterol 69(mg) Fat 8(g) Sodium 416(mg)

Butternut Squash Pie

My mother is famous for this simple, yet elegant pie, which, to me tastes like the essence of autumn.

9-inch **single pie crust** (see page 32)

1½ cups cooked, mashed **butternut squash**

½ cup **sugar**

1 tsp **ground cinnamon**

½ tsp **ground nutmeg**

¼ tsp **allspice**

½ tsp **salt**

3 **eggs**, beaten

1 cup **1% milk**

whipped cream (optional)

- Preheat oven to 400 degrees.
- In a bowl, combine squash, sugar, cinnamon, nutmeg, allspice, salt, and eggs.
- Mix well and stir in the milk.
- Pour filling into prepared pie crust.
- Bake for 30 to 35 minutes, until firm. Garnish with dollop of whipped cream if desired.

Serves 10. Each serving supplies:
Calories(kcal) 309 Protein 6(g) Carbohydrates 34(g) Dietary Fiber 2(g) Cholesterol 65(mg) Fat 16(g) Sodium 151(mg)

Butternut Squash à la Lena

It's no secret that sunny-hued butternut squash is a Hafner family favorite. This dish, created by my mother, is a nice change of pace. It highlights the savory rather than the sweet side of squash.

1 butternut squash, about 1½-2 pounds

Salt and pepper to taste

Topping

½ cup unseasoned breadcrumbs

1 T minced onion

¼ cup grated Romano cheese

½ tsp dried oregano

pinch dried basil

¼ cup chopped fresh parsley

1 T olive oil

- Preheat oven to 375 degrees.
- Peel squash and cut into 1-inch cubes. Place in medium saucepan and add water to cover. Cover pan, bring to a boil, reduce heat, and remove cover. Simmer for about 2 minutes, until squash is tender enough to pierce with a fork (but not mushy). Drain squash, reserving ½ cup liquid.
- Season squash with salt and pepper and place in bottom of 9-by-13-inch baking dish. Pour in reserved cooking liquid.
- In a small bowl, blend dry topping ingredients. Stir in oil and sprinkle mixture over squash.
- Bake for 20-30 minutes, until topping is lightly browned.

Serves 4-6. Each serving supplies:
Calories(kcal) 177 Protein 4(g) Carbohydrates 25(g) Dietary Fiber 5(g) Cholesterol 3(mg) Fat 8(g) Sodium 178(mg)

"Smashed" Potato Salad

This is my re-creation of a rustic potato salad served when my daughter Taryn graduated from culinary school. It's ideal for a tailgate or potluck, since it has no mayonnaise and tastes terrific at room temperature.

3½ pounds **new potatoes**, peeled and cut into quarters

Dressing

2 **cloves garlic**, minced

¼ cup finely chopped **sweet onion**

1 T chopped **fresh tarragon**

1 tsp **Dijon mustard**

⅓ cup **white balsamic vinegar**

⅔ cup **olive oil**

½ tsp **salt**

¼ tsp **ground pepper**

- Boil the potatoes until easily pierced by a fork, about 20 minutes.
- While the potatoes cook, prepare the dressing. In a small bowl, combine all ingredients EXCEPT olive oil. Slowly drizzle in oil, whisking constantly until the dressing is emulsified (or thoroughly blended with no oil separation).
- When the potatoes are tender, drain. With a potato masher, or a fork, mash gently until chunky — not smooth like mashed potatoes.
- Allow the potatoes to cool for 10 minutes and slowly fold in the dressing. Season with salt and pepper.
- Serve warm or at room temperature (but refrigerate if storing overnight).

Serves 12. Each serving supplies:
Calories(kcal) 224 Protein 2 (g) Carbohydrates 28 (g) Dietary Fiber 2 (g) Cholesterol 0 (mg) Fat 12 (g) Sodium 115 (mg)

[**For a dash of color, I like to use red potatoes, scrubbed and only partially peeled before cooking.**]

Cranberry Rice Pilaf

Studded with cranberry jewels and parsley flecks, this lovely rice instantly upgrades a simple entrée such as chicken or pork.

2 T olive oil

½ cup minced onion

2 cups fat-free, lower-sodium chicken broth

1 cup rice (uncooked)

½ cup chopped dried cranberries

2 T chopped Italian parsley

- Add oil to a medium saucepan (with lid) and place over medium heat. Add onion and sauté until translucent, about 5 minutes.
- Add chicken broth and rice to the saucepan, raise heat, and bring to a boil.
- Lower heat, stir cranberries into rice mixture, cover, and simmer for about 25 minutes until the rice absorbs the liquid. Spoon into a serving bowl and garnish with parsley.

Serves 4-6. Each serving supplies:
Calories(kcal) 246 Protein 4(g) Carbohydrates 44(g) Dietary Fiber 1(g) Cholesterol 0(mg) Fat 6(g) Sodium 234(mg)

Glorious Greens

Our American obsession with crisp, green salads tends to obscure a broader array of leafy, lovely, nutritious greens. Varieties such as chard, escarole, and kale are surprisingly mild in flavor, yet dense with vitamins and minerals. They may require a bit of cooking, but they're well worth a few minutes of your time.

A healthy head of greens can trap a surprising amount of dirt between its curly leaves. My strategy is to separate the leaves in a clean sink of cold water. I swish the leaves around to loosen the dirt, drain the water, refill the sink, and repeat the process, sometimes several times. When the leaves are pristine, and all the dirt has washed away, I drain and roughly chop the greens, then proceed with the recipe. If you don't have the time — or the inclination — to play in the sink, you can sometimes find pre-washed and pre-chopped greens at the supermarket.

Escarole Curly, tangy, and slightly bitter – it is the inspiration and foundation for CNY's famous Utica Greens.

Kale A cousin of cabbage and member of the cruciferous family. Peppery, rather bitter — and with its curly leaves — darn pretty.

Swiss Chard Sometimes sweet — and a bit salty — chard has a thick, crunchy (often colorful) stalk. So rich in nutrients it has been called "the valedictorian of vegetables."

Beet Greens Similar to Swiss chard in taste and texture, the edible, red-veined leaves of the beet are, hands down, the most nutritious part of the plant.

Spinach Surely the most familiar of greens, spinach is mild-tasting when eaten raw, more acidic when cooked. Tender "baby" leaves are best for salad.

Kale
Beet Greens
Red Swiss Chard
Spinach
Escarole

Crispy Kale

At first glance, this crunchy tangle of green gets a lot of quizzical looks. After one taste, those looks turn to smiles. This is a versatile recipe from my niece and kindred spirit Jill Garrick Pilger of Hamlet Organic Garden in Brookhaven, N.Y.

1 bunch **kale**, washed, stems removed

1 T **olive oil**

1 **clove garlic**, minced

Salt and pepper to taste

- Preheat oven to 500 degrees.
- Stack leaves, roll into cylinder and slice crosswise — or chiffonade — into strips ¼- to ½-inch in width.
- Transfer the strips to a bowl, add the olive oil and garlic, and toss with tongs. Season with salt and pepper. Continue to toss until strips are thoroughly coated with oil.
- Spread kale strips evenly across a large baking sheet. Transfer to preheated oven and bake until crispy, about 5 minutes. To prevent strips from burning, toss once or twice during baking.

Serves 4. Each serving supplies:
Calories(kcal) 64 Protein 2(g) Carbohydrates 7(g) Dietary Fiber 1(g) Cholesterol 0(mg) Fat 4(g) Sodium 29(mg)

[To transform this popular finger food into a light meal, simply top with fried or poached eggs.]

Linda's "Lite" Greens

If you're Italian and grew up in Central New York, you're probably familiar with Utica Greens, a legendary local favorite. I'm all for cooked greens, but I prefer to keep them simple — and healthy. My vegetarian version has so much flavor you won't miss the meat.

2 pounds fresh escarole, washed, trimmed, and chopped

¼ cup olive oil

½ cup chopped sweet onion

2 cloves garlic, minced

Red pepper flakes, if desired

Topping

½ cup unseasoned breadcrumbs

2 T grated Romano cheese

¼ tsp salt

1 T minced onion

1 T minced fresh parsley

1 T olive oil

- Add chopped escarole to a large pot and add 1 cup water. Bring to a boil over medium-high heat and cook until wilted, about 3-5 minutes. Remove from heat and drain.
- In a large ovenproof skillet, heat oil over medium flame. Add onion and garlic and gently sauté until translucent, about 5 minutes. Add escarole. Sauté until tender, about 5 minutes.
- Season with salt and pepper. Add red pepper flakes to taste, if desired.
- Turn on your oven's broiler. Transfer escarole mixture to a 2-quart baking dish if skillet is not ovenproof.
- Combine topping ingredients and sprinkle over escarole mixture.
- Place dish in oven and broil until breadcrumbs are lightly browned, watching carefully so they don't burn.

Serves 4-6. Each serving supplies:
Calories(kcal) 208 Protein 4(g) Carbohydrates 15(g) Dietary Fiber 6(g) Cholesterol 2(mg) Fat 15(g) Sodium 279(mg)

Swiss Chard with Raisins and Almonds

I'm pleased to share this recipe from my niece Jill Garrick Pilger. Jill, a registered dietitian, and her husband, Sean, operate Hamlet Organic Garden in Brookhaven, N.Y. It thrills me to see a new generation embrace the idea of a healthy, delicious diet.

2 T extra virgin olive oil, divided

½ large white onion sliced

¼ tsp paprika

2 pounds Swiss chard, coarsely chopped

½ cup golden raisins

½ cup water

¼ cup coarsely chopped almonds with skins

Salt and pepper to taste

- Place 1 tablespoon of oil in a 6-quart lidded pot and place over medium heat. Add onion and cook, stirring, until translucent, about 3 minutes.
- Sprinkle onion with paprika and continue to cook, stirring, for 1 minute. Add chard in small batches and continue to stir until wilted.
- Add raisins and water, cover, and cook, stirring occasionally, until chard is tender, about 7 minutes.
- Meanwhile, add remaining oil to a small, heavy skillet and place over medium-low heat. Add almonds and cook, stirring frequently, until golden, about 3 to 5 minutes.
- When chard is tender, remove from heat and season with salt and pepper. Transfer to serving bowl, sprinkle with almonds, and serve.

Serves 4. Each serving supplies:
Calories(kcal) 189 Protein 6(g) Carbohydrates 26(g) Dietary Fiber 6(g) Cholesterol 0(mg) Fat 9(g) Sodium 374(mg)

[**Instead of Swiss chard, you can substitute other leafy greens, such as spinach or kale. You can also turn this dish into a meal by simply adding crumbled goat cheese, feta, or even cooked quinoa.**]

Beet Greens with Orange Zest

This recipe is from my niece Emily Gelsomin, who is a registered dietitian at Massachusetts General Hospital, in Boston. It's no coincidence that so many of our family members are passionate about fresh, healthy food. You can follow the trail right back to my mother's kitchen and my father's garden.

2 T canola oil

4 cloves garlic, minced

2 bunches (about 1 pound) beet greens

1 orange, zested and juiced

½ cup raisins

¼ tsp cayenne pepper (optional)

Salt and pepper to taste

- Pour oil in a large skillet and place over medium-low heat. Toss in the garlic and sauté for about 1 to 2 minutes, watching carefully so garlic doesn't burn.
- Add beet greens to skillet and season with salt and pepper. Raise heat to medium and sauté until greens are wilted, about 3 to 5 minutes.
- Add orange zest, orange juice, raisins, and cayenne pepper (if desired). Continue to cook for 7 to 10 minutes until most of the liquid evaporates.
- Serve solo as a vegetable. For a quick meal, toss the hot greens with cooked pasta and crumbled goat cheese.

Serves 4. Each serving supplies:
Calories(kcal) 146 Protein 2(g) Carbohydrates 21(g)
Dietary Fiber 3(g) Cholesterol 0(mg) Fat 7(g) Sodium 146(mg)

Flounder with Mushrooms, Garlic, and Vermouth

Fish is a wonderful part of a healthy diet. It is high in protein and "good" fat. This recipe gets an additional nutritional boost from the vegetables — and it's all made in one pan.

4 T unsalted butter, divided

1 T olive oil

10 ounces white or baby bella mushrooms, wiped clean and sliced ½ -inch thick

1 red pepper, cut in strips

4 cloves garlic, minced

½ cup dry vermouth

3½ T chopped fresh parsley, divided

1 T white balsamic vinegar

½ tsp salt

½ tsp freshly ground black pepper

4 (6 oz) flounder fillets, skinned

- In a heavy skillet melt 3 tablespoons of butter over medium-high heat. Add the mushrooms and red pepper. Sauté 5 to 7 minutes, stirring occasionally. Add the garlic. Stir until golden and fragrant, about 45 seconds. Pour in vermouth, parsley, vinegar, salt, and pepper. Boil until the liquid is reduced by half, about 2 minutes.
- Remove skillet from heat. Season flounder with salt and pepper. Nestle fillets in skillet, tucking tails under if necessary to even out thickness. Spoon a few of the mushrooms over the fish.
- Return skillet to stove over medium heat. Bring to a gentle simmer, cover, reduce to medium low, and continue to simmer until just cooked, about 7-12 minutes depending on thickness. Using a slotted spatula, transfer fish to serving dish.
- Over low heat, whisk remaining 1 tablespoon butter into the pan with the mushrooms and peppers. Spoon over the fish. Garnish with the remaining ½ tablespoon of parsley.

Serves 4. Each serving supplies:
Calories(kcal) 329 Protein 8(g) Carbohydrates 30(g) Dietary Fiber 1(g) Cholesterol 110(mg) Fat 17 (g) Sodium 430(mg)

Add a nutritional punch by serving this fish on a bed of spinach.

“Spaghetti” Sauce

I know that summer is nearly over when I feel the urge to make this tomato sauce. In my mother’s kitchen, it was a Sunday ritual – but not an all-day ordeal. Our family’s traditional red sauce cooks for about an hour, just long enough for the tomatoes to absorb the flavors of the meatballs and sausage.

4 (28 oz) cans whole, peeled plum tomatoes

1 tsp salt

pepper to taste

1 tsp sugar

1 tsp dried basil

1 pound Italian sausage rope

2 pounds meatballs, browned well (see next recipe)

[For extra flavor I sometimes add browned, boneless spareribs with the rest of the meat.]

- One can at a time, empty tomatoes into a blender and briefly puree. Do not liquefy. Transfer tomatoes to 12-quart stockpot. Stir in salt, pepper, sugar, and basil.
- Brown sausage rope in a large skillet over medium-high heat. Remove sausage from skillet and drain on paper towels. Cut into 2-inch lengths.
- Add sausage and meatballs to the stockpot with tomatoes.
- Place stockpot over medium heat and cook sauce for 1 hour, stirring occasionally – and carefully, so that meatballs remain intact.
- May be stored in the refrigerator (for up to 3 days) or frozen. Gently reheat sauce over low heat.

Serves 8-10. Each serving supplies:
Calories(kcal) 515 Protein 37(g) Carbohydrates 33(g) Dietary Fiber 4(g) Cholesterol 170 (mg) Fat 24(g) Sodium 2056(mg)

[In early autumn, the season’s last tomatoes often cover my kitchen counters. Making this sauce is a great way to clear some space! I simply drop the tomatoes into boiling water for a few minutes, slip off the skins and proceed with the recipe.]

My Mother's Meatballs

2 pounds ground beef (95 percent lean)

4 large eggs

½ cup white onion, chopped

2 cloves garlic, minced

¼ cup fresh Italian parsley, chopped

1 T fresh chopped basil, chopped (or 1 tsp dried)

1⅓ cups unseasoned breadcrumbs

2 tsp salt

1 tsp ground black pepper

1 cup grated Romano cheese

1 cup 1% milk

1 cup olive oil (for frying the meatballs)

- In large bowl, combine all ingredients (except oil) and mix well. Form mixture into balls, 1½ inches in diameter.
- Pour the oil into a 12-inch skillet, ideally with slanted slides. Place over medium-high heat. When the oil is hot, add the meatballs and brown on all sides, allowing each side to "harden" before turning.
- Before adding the browned meatballs to the sauce, drain well on paper towels.

Makes 32 meatballs

Calories(kcal) 95 Protein 8(g) Carbohydrates 4(g) Dietary Fiber 0(g) Cholesterol 44(mg) Fat 5(g) Sodium 261(mg)

[If the meatballs are headed straight for the sauce, they should be thoroughly browned and almost crispy on the outside — to keep them from falling apart — but not necessarily cooked through. They'll continue to cook with the sauce.]

White Chili

When you need a tasty, hearty dinner that's ready in a flash, this chili fills the bill. With leftover cooked chicken on hand, you can have it on the table in 25 minutes or less. I often make a batch or two ahead of time, freeze it, and just reheat it when we're river rafting or camping. Add a salad and Italian bread, and you have a meal.

2 cans (15 oz) **Great Northern beans**, rinsed and drained

2 packages (10 oz) **frozen sweet corn**

2 cans (14 oz) **fat free, lower-sodium chicken broth**

3 **cloves garlic**, minced

1 cup chopped **white onion**

2 small cans (5.75oz) chopped **green chilies**, drained

2 tsp **ground cumin**

¼ tsp **ground cloves**

¼ cup **dry white wine** (optional)

1 T chopped **fresh cilantro**

4 cups **cooked chicken**, shredded or cut in pieces

Garnish

1 cup shredded **Monterey Jack** or cheddar cheese

¼ cup additional chopped **fresh cilantro**

- In a large pot, combine all ingredients except chicken and cheese. Place pot over medium heat and simmer for about 15 minutes. Add the chicken and cook until heated through – no longer.
- Ladle the chili into individual bowls and top with shredded cheese and chopped cilantro.

Serves 6. Each serving supplies:
Calories(kcal) 482 Protein 42(g) Carbohydrates 54(g) Dietary Fiber 13(g) Cholesterol 78(mg) Fat 10(g) Sodium 995(mg)

Cuban Pork with Black Beans and Rice

Our niece and one-time Floridian, Lisa, introduced this crowd-pleaser at a huge Hafner family reunion. The citrus-infused pork tickles the palate and spares the chef by simmering all day in the crockpot.

2½ pounds boneless pork roast *

Linda's MoJo Marinade

1 white onion, chopped
2 T minced garlic
2 cups orange juice
1 T fresh lemon juice
4 T fresh lime juice
1 tsp ground cumin
1 tsp ground coriander
2 tsp dried oregano
1 tsp ground black pepper
2 tsp salt

- Cut the pork roast into 2-inch squares and layer in the crockpot.
- In a small bowl, combine the marinade ingredients and pour over the pork.
- Set the crock pot on low for 8 hours.
- Before serving, shred the pork with two forks. Serve with Black Beans and Rice (below).

Serves 10. Each serving supplies:
(without beans and rice) Calories(kcal) 129 Protein 21(g) Carbohydrates 0(g) Dietary Fiber 0(g) Cholesterol 64(mg) Fat 4(g) Sodium 51(mg). (Please note: Marinade is not included in the nutritional analysis.)

Black Beans and Rice

2 cans black beans, rinsed and drained
1 T olive oil
½ cup finely chopped onion
1 red bell pepper, finely chopped
2 cups rice, cooked just before serving

- Place oil in a large skillet over medium heat. Add onion and bell pepper and sauté until soft, about 5 minutes.
- Add beans and warm through.
- Serve beans over cooked rice.

Serves 10. Each serving supplies:
Calories(kcal) 235 Protein 8(g) Carbohydrates 47(g) Dietary Fiber 6(g) Cholesterol 0(mg) Fat 5(g) Sodium 313(mg)

[*Pork shoulder can be substituted for the boneless pork roast. It's lower in cost but unfortunately not as lean.]

Apple Country's Signature Apples

Red Delicious An excellent snack or salad apple. Sweet taste with crisp, yellow flesh. Thick-skinned and stores well.

Empire A sweet-tart cross between the popular Red Delicious and McIntosh apples. Great for lunch boxes, since it resists bruising. Also good for applesauce and baking.

Cortland Firm and famous for its snow-white flesh. Great for salads and baking.

McIntosh Sweet, juicy, and tender-fleshed. Great for eating but breaks down quickly in cooking and baking.

Macoun Extra-sweet, juicy, and tender, this New-York native is excellent for eating, salads, and applesauce.

Northern Spy Prized for its inner beauty, this firm, tart apple is perfect for pies, desserts, and cider.

Ida Red An all-around apple that's not too sweet and not too firm. It's great for eating yet holds its own in pies and applesauce.

Granny Smith Discovered in Australia and popular worldwide, it's very tart and versatile — equally good for snacking or baking.

Fresh, Simple, Healthy Recipe

Applesauce

6 ripe apples (any variety or combination)

½ cup water, apple cider or **apple juice**

1 tsp ground cinnamon (optionall)

Serves 4-6. Each serving supplies:
Calories(kcal) 74 Protein 0(g) Carbohydrates 20(g)
Dietary Fiber 2(g) Cholesterol 0(mg) Fat 0(g)
Sodium 1(mg)

- Peel and slice apples into large pieces. Transfer to a lidded, medium-size saucepan and add water, cider, or apple juice.
- Place pan over medium heat and cook, covered, until apples are very soft.
- Remove pan from heat and stir in cinnamon. For chunky applesauce, mash with a potato masher. For a very smooth consistency, transfer to a food processor and puree.

Simple and simply delicious, this homemade applesauce is so easy you'll wonder why you ever bought it in a jar — especially since we live in the middle of Apple Country!

Apple Country Cake

Here in Apple Country, every family seems to have a cherished apple cake recipe. This moist, heart-healthy version is a fall favorite with my family.

½ cup sugar

½ tsp ground cinnamon

¾ cup chopped walnuts, divided

4 cups apples, peeled and diced

1 cup sugar

1½ cups flour

1½ tsp baking powder

½ tsp salt

2 eggs, well beaten

¾ cup low-fat milk

¼ cup butter, melted

¼ cup canola oil

Confectioner's sugar, for dusting

- Preheat oven to 350 degrees.
- In a small bowl, mix together sugar, cinnamon, and ½ cup walnuts.
- Grease a 9-by-13-inch pan and fill with diced apples. Sprinkle apples with cinnamon mixture.
- In a bowl, stir together the flour, sugar, baking powder, and salt.
- In a larger bowl, combine the eggs, milk, butter, and oil. Add the flour mixture and combine until smooth.
- Pour the batter over apples, allowing time for it to settle between the apples. Sprinkle with remaining nuts.
- Bake for about 1 hour or until a toothpick comes out clean.
- Before serving, lightly sift powdered sugar over top of cake.

Serves 12. Each serving supplies:
Calories(kcal) 318 Protein 4(g) Carbohydrates 45(g) Dietary Fiber 2(g) Cholesterol 46(mg) Fat 14(g) Sodium 206(mg)

If the apples are sweet, there's no need to sprinkle them with sugar before adding the cake batter.

Baked Apples

Absolutely simple, fresh, and healthy!

4 apples (such as Northern Spy or Ida Red)

½ cup raisins

¼ cup chopped walnuts

¼ cup maple syrup or brown sugar

½ cup apple cider, apple juice, or water

- Preheat oven to 350 degrees.
- Core and peel a strip around the middle of each apple to prevent from bursting in the oven.
- Stuff raisins and walnuts into the center of each apple.
- If using maple syrup, drizzle into the core of each apple. If using brown sugar, divide evenly among the 4 apples and sprinkle over filling.
- Place the apples upright in an 8-by-8-inch baking dish. Pour the apple cider, apple juice, or water into bottom of the pan.
- Bake for about 45 minutes or until apples are very soft when pierced with a fork.

Serves 4. Each serving supplies:
Calories(kcal) 263 Protein 2(g) Carbohydrates 57(g) Dietary Fiber 6(g) Cholesterol 0(mg) Fat 5(g) Sodium 7(mg)

With Northern Spy or Ida Red apples, you can skip the maple syrup or brown sugar. These late-season apples are plenty sweet on their own.

Winter: The Comfort Season

As black-and-white as it often seems, winter is ripe with culinary promise. What season is more synonymous with holiday delicacies and treasured family recipes? When are citrus fruits more vibrant and welcome? Where could it be more tempting to simmer, stew, roast, and bake than in frigid Central New York, under a blanket of snow?

At this time of year, I forage for ingredients from a variety of sources. By reaching into my freezer, I can concoct a fruit cobbler that rivals any sumptuous summer dessert. In my pantry are the makings of a superfast, supercharged vodka sauce. Our local supermarkets offer a truly global array of fresh fruits and vegetables. But in winter, as in summer, I try to keep my food sources as close to home as possible. I'm more comfortable serving fresh produce from Florida and California than from another country. The farther our food travels, the more likely it's been harvested early or chemically treated. What's the point of eating exotic, out-of-season delicacies that taste like cardboard or carry toxins to the table? I think it's more rewarding to add an unexpected seasoning (like cinnamon) to an everyday staple (like chicken), as in my daughter's irresistible recipe for Moroccan Chicken. And as a last resort — when our patience with winter is wearing very thin — we can always count on chocolate, which knows no season and never fails to delight.

Winter

Healthy Granola

One of the first wholesome health foods to hit the market in the 1960s, crunchy granola soon became a mainstream staple. I love it layered with fruit in a yogurt parfait — perfect for special Sundays and houseguests.

4 cups oatmeal (not instant)

½ cup raw wheat germ

½ cup sesame seeds, unhulled

1 cup coarsely chopped raw almonds with skins

¼ cup chopped walnuts

½ cup honey or maple syrup

2 T canola oil

1 tsp vanilla extract

1 tsp ground cinnamon

½ cup chopped dried apricots

½ cup dried cranberries

- Preheat the oven to 350 degrees and lightly spray a large, shallow pan with cooking spray.
- In a large bowl, mix together all ingredients except the dried fruit.
- Transfer the mixture to a sheet pan and bake for 30 to 35 minutes, stirring occasionally, until golden.
- Remove granola from the oven and cool. Add dried fruits. Transfer to a sealed container and store in a cool, dry place for up to three weeks.

Serves 16. Each serving supplies:
Calories(kcal) 200 Protein 5(g) Carbohydrates 32(g) Dietary Fiber 4(g) Cholesterol 0(mg) Fat (7g) Sodium 2(mg)

Orange Sunburst Salad

This super-simple salad – which my grandmother made for us every winter – reminds me to celebrate something we often take for granted: sweet, sunny oranges in a dark, snowy season.

3 navel oranges

1 T olive oil

Freshly ground black pepper

- Peel the oranges, removing as much pith as possible. (The pith is the outer white layer beneath the skin.)
- Slice the oranges about ¼-inch thick and arrange them on a serving plate. Lightly drizzle the sliced oranges with olive oil and sprinkle with black pepper, coarsely ground.

Serves 6. Each serving supplies:
Calories(kcal) 54 Protein 1(g) Carbohydrates 9(g) Dietary Fiber 2(g) Cholesterol 0(mg) Fat 2(g) Sodium 1(mg)

Lucky Lentil Soup

Since lentils are shaped like little coins, Italians believe that sipping lentil soup on New Year's Eve brings good fortune. I believe that lentil soup brings even greater riches, in the form of good health.

1 pound **dried lentils**

8 cups **water**

2 **carrots**, peeled and chopped

1 **onion**, chopped

1 **celery rib**, chopped

1 cup **crushed tomatoes**

2 T **olive oil**

Salt and **pepper** to taste

- Rinse and sort through the lentils, discarding any stones or debris. Pour the lentils into an 8-quart saucepan.
- Add the water, carrots, onion, celery, tomatoes, and olive oil.
- Bring the mixture to a boil, lower the heat, and simmer, uncovered, until the lentils are tender, about 45 to 60 minutes. If the soup is too thick, add more water.
- Season with salt and pepper and serve.

Serves 8. Each serving supplies:
Calories(kcal) 244 Protein 16(g) Carbohydrates 39(g) Dietary Fiber 14(g) Cholesterol 0(mg) Fat 4(g) Sodium 74(mg)

[To turn this hearty soup into dinner, simply add a salad, fresh fruit, and Italian bread. For meat lovers, add ½ cup chopped ham or cooked turkey sausage.]

"Green" Split Pea Soup

I'm not a vegetarian, but I'm all for vegetables taking center stage. This hearty soup is delicious without meat, but you can easily add a hambone to the pot with the water. Or stir in ½ cup of chopped ham about 15 minutes before the soup is finished cooking.

1 pound dried split peas

1 T olive oil

1 large onion, chopped

1 T minced garlic (optional)

8 cups water

1 cup diced carrot

½ cup diced celery

1 bay leaf

Salt and pepper

- Rinse and sort through the peas, discarding any small stones or debris.
- Add the oil to an 8-quart saucepan and place over medium heat. Add the onion and sauté for about 5 minutes. Add the garlic, if using, and cook for 1 minute.
- Add the water, carrot, celery, peas, and bay leaf. Bring the mixture to a boil, lower the heat and simmer for 45 to 60 minutes, until the peas are soft.
- Season with salt and pepper.

Serves 8. Each serving supplies:
Calories(kcal) 195 Protein 12(g) Carbohydrates 33(g) Dietary Fiber 12(g) Cholesterol 0(mg) Fat 2(g) Sodium 29(mg)

Magical Chicken Soup

Scientists recently confirmed what grandmothers have long claimed — that chicken soup helps fight cold germs. Not that you need to justify a pot of chicken soup. It's soul food on a spoon!

1 whole chicken, 3 to 4 pounds

6 quarts water

2 T salt

½ tsp pepper

2 cups diced carrots

1 cup diced celery

½ cup chopped celery leaves

1 cup chopped onion

½ cup chopped Italian parsley, plus extra for garnish

- Thoroughly rinse the chicken, inside and out. Discard the giblets. Place the chicken in a large stockpot and add the water, salt, and pepper.
- Over medium heat, bring the water to a boil and continue to gently boil the chicken, uncovered, for about an hour, or until the meat seems ready to slip from the bones. Skim and discard any foam that surfaces as the water boils.
- Carefully remove the chicken from the pot and set aside to cool.
- If necessary, strain the soup to remove small bone fragments that might have slipped into the liquid.
- Add the vegetables to the soup and cook over medium heat until tender, about 20 minutes, until chicken is cool enough to handle. Remove and shred meat and return it to the soup. Season and serve.

Serves 16. Each serving supplies:
Calories(kcal) 120 Protein 13(g) Carbohydrates 3(g) Dietary Fiber 1(g) Cholesterol 38(mg) Fat 6(g) Sodium 951(mg)

Super Bowl Chili

Spain, Mexico, and the state of Texas all lay claim to the mouthwatering stew known as chili con carne. I can't testify to its origins, but I know that chili is a huge crowd pleaser on Super Bowl (or any chilly) Sunday.

1 pound **lean ground beef**

1 pound **ground turkey**

1 pound **Italian-style turkey sausage**, removed from casing

1 large **onion**, chopped

3 **bell peppers**, chopped (I like to mix red, orange, and yellow)

2 **cloves garlic**, minced

1 T **dried oregano**

1 tsp **ground cumin**

1 tsp **ground coriander**

¼ tsp **ground allspice**

¼ tsp **ground cloves**

1 (28 oz) can **diced tomatoes**

2 (15 oz) cans **tomato sauce**

1 T **brown sugar**

4 T **chili powder**

2 (4 oz) cans **chopped green chilies**

2 (15 oz) cans **kidney beans**, drained and rinsed

Salt and pepper to taste

[To add even more texture — and color — I like to serve chili with guacamole, low-fat sour cream or plain yogurt, grated Monterey Jack cheese, and chopped onion.]

- Place a large heavy-bottomed pot over medium-high heat and brown the meat, in batches if necessary.
- Reduce the heat to medium and stir in the onion, peppers, garlic, oregano, cumin, coriander, allspice, and cloves. Add the tomatoes and tomato sauce.
- Stir in the brown sugar, chili powder, green chilies, and kidney beans.
- Lower the heat, cover the pot, and simmer for 1 hour. (The chili may also be transferred to a crockpot and cooked on low heat for 3 hours.) Season with salt and pepper.

Serves 12. Each serving supplies:
Calories(kcal) 288 Protein 27(g) Carbohydrates 25(g) Dietary Fiber 8(g) Cholesterol 78(mg) Fat 9(g) Sodium 1,081(mg)

Crock Pot Beef Stew

A deep-flavored, slow-simmered beef stew is the essence of comfort food. My crock pot technique makes this cozy meal manageable even when the cook has a hectic schedule.

3 pounds **boneless beef chuck**, trimmed and cut into 1½ inch cubes

¼ cup **flour**

¼ cup **canola oil**

⅓ cup **tomato paste**

1 large **onion**, chopped

4-5 large **potatoes**, peeled and cut into 1-inch cubes

2 cups sliced **carrots** (1-inch slices) or 1 pound peeled baby carrots

3 cups **beef broth**, (fat-free, lower-sodium)

1 tsp **salt**

¼ tsp **ground black pepper**

1 tsp **dried thyme** (fresh is even better)

2 **bay leaves**

1 cup **frozen peas**, thawed

- Coat the beef cubes with flour. Pour the oil into a large skillet and place over medium-high heat. Add the beef and brown on all sides, in batches if necessary.
- Transfer the beef to a crock pot. Add the onion, potatoes, carrots, beef broth, salt, pepper, thyme, bay leaves, and tomato paste (everything but the peas).
- Cover the crock pot and cook on high heat for 4 to 6 hours (or on low for 8 hours).
- Stir the peas into the stew and heat through. Discard the bay leaves and serve.

Serves 10. Each serving supplies:
Calories(kcal) 386 Protein 33(g) Carbohydrates 37(g) Dietary Fiber 5(g) Cholesterol 59(mg) Fat 12(g) Sodium 536(mg)

Cod with Potatoes

Thanks to my Italian family, I grew up eating plenty of fresh fish. This pretty red-and-white casserole is a great way to introduce your family to the mild, clean taste of cod – and to the healthy habit of eating fish.

- 5 T **olive oil**
- ½ cup **onion**, chopped
- 2 **cloves garlic**, minced
- 1 (28 oz) can **whole plum tomatoes**
- ½ tsp **sugar**
- 2 tsp **fresh basil**, chopped
- 2 T **fresh Italian parsley**, chopped
- 1½ pounds **potatoes**, peeled
- **Salt** and **freshly ground black pepper**, to taste
- 2 T grated **Romano cheese**
- 1½ pounds **fresh cod fillets**

- Preheat oven to 400 degrees.

Make the tomato sauce

- Add 4 tablespoons of oil to a medium saucepan over medium heat. Add the onion and garlic and sauté until translucent, about 5 minutes. Watch the garlic so it doesn't burn.
- Meanwhile, pour the tomatoes with their juice into a blender and puree until roughly chopped. Transfer 2 cups of the chopped tomatoes to the saucepan. (Reserve the rest for another use.)
- Add the sugar, basil, and 1 tablespoon parsley to the saucepan and simmer the tomato sauce, over medium heat, for 10 minutes.

Prepare the potatoes

- Slice the potatoes ¼-inch thick. Layer the slices in the bottom of 9-x-13-inch baking dish that has been coated with cooking spray. Season the potatoes with salt and pepper.
- Spoon 1¼ cups of the tomato sauce over the potatoes, mixing lightly. Sprinkle with 1 tablespoon cheese. Cover with foil and bake for 30 minutes, or until the potatoes are easily pierced with a fork. Remove the potatoes from the oven and uncover.

Add the cod

- Layer the cod fillets on top of the potatoes. Season with salt and pepper. Spoon the remaining ¾ cup tomato sauce over the cod. Sprinkle with remaining parsley and cheese. Drizzle with 1 tablespoon oil.
- Return the dish to the oven and bake for 15 minutes or until the cod flakes when cut with a fork.

Serves 4-6. Each serving supplies:
Calories(kcal) 388 Protein 26(g) Carbohydrates 36(g) Dietary Fiber 4(g) Cholesterol 53(mg) Fat 15(g) Sodium 376(mg)

Sea Scallops Supreme

Home cooks often overlook succulent sea scallops. In fact, they couldn't be easier to prepare — or more elegant to serve.

1 pound **fresh sea scallops**

Marinade

½ cup **dry white wine** or dry vermouth

1 T **olive oil**

1 clove **garlic**, minced

2 T chopped **fresh Italian parsley**

Topping

½ cup **fresh breadcrumbs**

1 tsp **olive oil**

- Rinse scallops and pat dry with paper towel. If desired, cut scallops in half.
- Place the scallops in a 9-by-13 inch baking dish.
- In a small bowl, combine the marinade ingredients. Pour the marinade over the scallops. Cover and refrigerate for 1 hour.
- When ready to cook, preheat broiler. Remove scallops from marinade and arrange in a shallow ovenproof dish with sides.
- Broil the scallops for 3 minutes. Remove from broiler, turn, and sprinkle with the breadcrumbs. Return to oven and broil for 3 more minutes.

Serves 4. Each serving supplies:
Calories(kcal) 125 Protein 19(g) Carbohydrates 6(g) Dietary Fiber 0(g) Cholesterol 37(mg) Fat 2(g) Sodium 221(mg)
(Please note: Marinade is not included in the nutritional analysis.)

[To make fresh breadcrumbs, place a slice of bread in your food processor and pulse.]

Four-Season London Broil

A good steak knows no season – it's as welcome in a snowstorm as it is in barbecue weather. In the winter, just slip the steak under the broiler, or keep your gas grill by the kitchen door.

1½ pound flank steak or boneless sirloin

Marinade

2 tsp salt

1 tsp black pepper

1 T fresh basil

1 T fresh rosemary (or 1 tsp dried rosemary)

1 clove garlic

½ cup onion, chopped

2 T wine vinegar

2 T canola oil

- Combine marinade ingredients in a shallow dish. Slip the steak into the dish and turn to coat both sides with the marinade. Let stand for 2 hours or refrigerate overnight.
- When ready to cook, turn on the broiler. Remove the steak from the marinade and transfer to a broiling pan. Broil the steak 3 inches from heat for 5 minutes. Turn steak and brush the other side with a little marinade. Broil for an additional 4 minutes.
- To serve, slice the steak diagonally (across the grain) as thinly as possible.

Serves 4-6. Each serving supplies:
Calories(kcal) 261 Protein 38(g) Carbohydrates 0(g) Dietary Fiber 0(g) Cholesterol 61(mg) Fat 11(g) Sodium 76(mg)
(Please note: Marinade is not included in the nutritional analysis.)

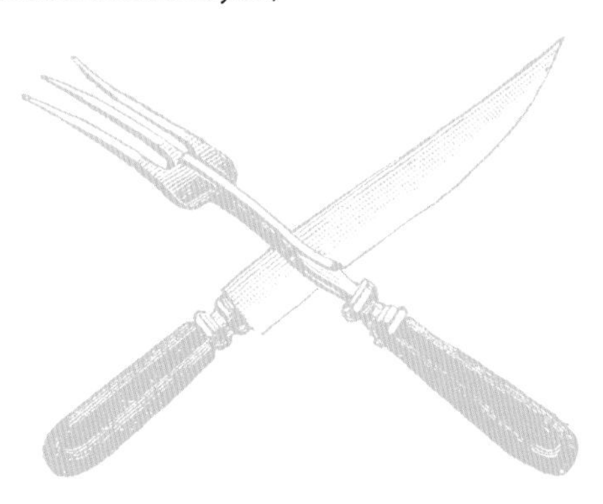

Pronto Vodka Sauce

In the dead of winter – when fresh, local tomatoes are a faint memory – this pantry-sourced sauce delivers an unexpected jolt of flavor.

2 T olive oil

1 cup chopped onion

4 cloves garlic, minced

½ cup lean chopped ham or prosciutto (optional)

¼ cup red wine vinegar or balsamic vinegar

½ cup vodka

1 T sugar

2 T tomato paste

¼ tsp freshly ground black pepper

2 (14.5 oz) cans diced tomatoes

½ cup half-and-half

2 T chopped fresh Italian parsley

½ cup grated Parmesan or Romano cheese

1 pound ziti or penne pasta

- Pour the oil into a large saucepan over medium heat. Add the onion, garlic and, if desired, ham or prosciutto. Sauté until soft, about 5 minutes, taking care not to burn the garlic.
- Stir in the vinegar, vodka, sugar, tomato paste, pepper, and diced tomatoes.
- Bring the mixture to a boil, reduce the heat, and simmer, uncovered, for about 20 minutes. Remove from the heat and stir in the half-and-half and parsley.
- Meanwhile, cook the pasta according to package directions. Drain and toss with grated cheese. Divide the pasta among shallow serving bowls, top with the sauce, and garnish with additional parsley.

Serves 4-6. Each serving supplies:
Calories(kcal) 570 Protein 18(g) Carbohydrates 85(g) Dietary Fiber 5(g) Cholesterol 16(mg) Fat 12(g) Sodium 462(mg)

Taryn's Moroccan Chicken

My daughter Taryn has a flair for combining slightly exotic accents and familiar comfort foods. This slow-simmered chicken makes a perfect winter supper.

8 **skinless, boneless chicken thighs**

1 tsp **ground cinnamon**

½ tsp **ground ginger**

1 T **olive oil**

1 **onion**, sliced

3 **cloves garlic**, minced

2 cups **fat free, lower-sodium chicken broth**

½ cup chopped **Kalamata olives**, pitted

½ cup chopped **green olives**, pitted

1 **lemon**, juiced and zested

½ cup chopped **fresh cilantro**

- Dust chicken with cinnamon and ginger.
- Heat the olive oil in a large frying pan over medium-high heat. Add the chicken and brown on all sides. Remove chicken and set aside.
- In the same frying pan, sauté the onion and garlic over medium heat until soft and lightly browned. Add the chicken stock to the frying pan, stirring to incorporate any browned bits.
- Return the chicken to the frying pan. Add the olives. Reduce the heat to low and simmer, covered, for about 40 minutes, until the chicken is cooked through.
- Remove the pan from the heat and stir in the lemon juice, lemon zest, and cilantro.

Number of Servings: 4-6. Each serving supplies:
Calories (kcal) 279 Protein 24(g) Carbohydrates 7(g) Dietary Fiber 1(g) Cholesterol 79(mg)
Fat 17(g) Sodium 720(mg)

[My daughter, Taryn, serves this over couscous, which she "spikes" by adding a little ground cinnamon and a few cinnamon sticks to the cooking water.]

In-a-Pinch Clam Spaghetti

This is what's known as a pantry dish, made from ingredients we routinely have on hand. At our house, it has saved the day dozens of times.

4 (6.5 oz) cans **minced** or **chopped clams**, with juice

¼ cup **olive oil**

3 **cloves garlic**, minced

½ cup **dry white wine**

¼ cup chopped **fresh parsley**

Dried oregano, optional

Crushed **hot pepper flakes**, optional

1 pound **dried pasta (preferably cappellini)**

½ cup grated **Parmesan cheese**

- Drain the clams and reserve the juice.
- Add the oil to a skillet and place over medium heat. Add the garlic and gently sauté, until it begins to sizzle and becomes fragrant. Be careful not to burn the garlic, or it will make the sauce bitter.
- Add the wine and reserved clam juice. Reduce heat slightly and simmer for 8 minutes. If desired, add a pinch of dried oregano and crushed hot pepper to taste.
- Cook the pasta al dente, according to package directions.
- While the pasta is cooking, add the clams and parsley to the skillet and cook gently over low heat. If you add the clams earlier – or cook them at a higher temperature – they will become rubbery.
- Drain the pasta and transfer it to a large serving bowl. Toss the pasta with ½ cup of liquid from clam sauce to blend the flavors. Add the remaining sauce with clams and ¼ cup of the cheese.
- Serve immediately, garnished with the remaining cheese.

Number of Servings: 6-8. Each serving supplies:
Calories (kcal) 380 Protein 19(g) Carbohydrates 50(g) Dietary Fiber 2 (g) Cholesterol 24(mg) Fat 11(g) Sodium 782

Chicken Cacciatore

A cacciatore, or "hunter's stew", traditionally features tomatoes. In my family's version, the focus is on mushrooms, which hungry hunters found by foraging in the woods.

1 pound **chicken thighs**, boneless and skinless

1 pound **chicken legs**, skinless

Salt and **pepper** to taste

2 T **olive oil**

1 cup diced **onion**

½ cup diced **celery**

2 cups sliced **fresh mushrooms**

¼ cup chopped **fresh parsley**

¼ cup chopped **fresh basil**

½ cup **dry white wine**, such as **pinot grigio**

- Rinse the chicken pieces and pat dry with paper towels. Season with salt and pepper.
- Pour the oil into a large skillet and place over medium-high heat. Add the chicken and brown for about 5 minutes, turning it to brown all sides.
- Add the onion, celery, mushrooms, parsley, and basil to skillet. Sauté, stirring, until softened, about 5 minutes.
- Pour in the wine, lower the heat, cover, and simmer for 15 minutes or until the chicken is cooked through.

Serves 4-6. Each serving supplies:
Calories(kcal) 330 Protein 36(g) Carbohydrates 5(g) Dietary Fiber 1(g) Cholesterol 132(mg) Fat 16(g) Sodium 151(mg)

Oven Chicken and Potatoes

This is a simple dinner you can throw together and have on the table in less than an hour! It's a quickie I rely on regularly.

4 or 5 **medium potatoes** cut into small wedges (for extra nutrition, scrub the skin and partially peel)

4 or 5 **carrots** peeled and cut into wedges similar in size to the potato wedges

1 **small chicken**, cut up or use your favorite combination of breasts, legs, and/or thighs

The Sauce

2 T **olive oil**

1 tsp **dried basil**

½ tsp **dried oregano**

1 **clove garlic**, chopped fine

1 **small onion**, chopped fine

Salt and pepper, to taste

- Preheat oven to 400 degrees.
- Mix together the sauce ingredients with a small whisk or fork.
- Toss the potatoes and carrots with half the sauce. Pour into a 9-x-13-inch pan, spread evenly. Toss the chicken pieces in the remaining sauce. Place chicken in one layer over the vegetables. Cover tightly with aluminum foil and bake 45 minutes.
- Remove the cover and bake about 15 minutes more or until everything is thoroughly cooked and golden brown.
- Variation: When you remove the cover, brush the chicken with your favorite barbecue sauce.

Serves 4-6. Each serving supplies:
Calories(kcal) 484 Protein 37(g) Carbohydrates 34(g) Dietary Fiber 4(g) Cholesterol 105(mg) Fat 22(g) Sodium 149(mg)

Freezer Fruit Cobbler

At the height of summer, I stock my freezer with fresh blueberries, raspberries, strawberries, and peaches. In the depths of winter, I love to revisit those bright summer tastes and textures with this simple, cozy cobbler.

4 cups **frozen fruit**

½ cup **sugar** (less if the fruit is sweet)

2 T **cornstarch**

Crust

4 ounces **butter**, softened

¾ cup **sugar**

1 **egg**, lightly beaten

1 cup **flour**

1 tsp **baking powder**

½ tsp **baking soda**

- Preheat the oven to 325 degrees.
- Scatter the fruit in an 8-by-8-inch baking dish. Combine the sugar and cornstarch and sprinkle over fruit.
- To prepare the crust, combine the flour, baking powder, and baking soda in a small bowl and set aside.
- In a medium bowl, combine the butter and sugar. Stir in the egg. Gradually add the flour mixture. The batter will seem quite stiff — somewhere between a heavy cake batter and a light biscuit dough.
- Drop the batter, one spoonful at a time, over the top of the fruit. The batter will settle into the fruit as it bakes.
- Transfer the cobbler to the oven and bake for 60 minutes, until the top is lightly browned and cooked through.

Serves 12. Each serving supplies:
Calories(kcal) 223 Protein 2(g) Carbohydrates 36(g) Dietary Fiber 2(g) Cholesterol 38(mg) Fat 8(g) Sodium 154(mg)

Night-Shift French Toast Soufflé

When the occasion calls for an elegant breakfast or brunch – but the holiday chef is already running on empty – this overnight soufflé saves the day!

10 cups hearty, **whole-grain bread**, cut into 1-inch cubes (I use Pepperidge Farm 15-grain bread, about 16 slices)

8 ounces **cream cheese**, softened (lower-fat)

8 **large eggs**

1½ cups **1% milk**

⅔ cup **half-and-half**

½ cup **maple syrup**

½ tsp **vanilla extract**

2 T **powdered sugar**

Additional **maple syrup** for serving

- Place the bread cubes in a 13-x-9-inch baking dish that's been coated with cooking spray.
- Beat the cream cheese until smooth. Add the eggs one at a time, mixing well after each addition. Add the milk, half-and-half, ½ cup maple syrup, and vanilla, and mix until smooth. Pour this mixture over the bread cubes, cover the dish securely, and refrigerate overnight.
- About 1½ hours before serving, preheat the oven to 375 degrees.
- Remove the bread mixture from the refrigerator and let stand at room temperature for about 30 minutes.
- Bake for about 50 minutes or until set.
- Remove from oven and dust the top of the soufflé with powdered sugar. Serve with maple syrup.

Serves 12. Each serving supplies:
Calories(kcal) 289 Protein 14(g) Carbohydrates 41(g) Dietary Fiber 5(g) Cholesterol 158(mg) Fat 11(g) Sodium 309(mg)

New-Age Eggnog

You may consider eggnog an old-school tradition, but my son — while working on a television show in L.A. — made this eggnog for a Hollywood holiday party, and the celebrities swooned!

2 cups **half-and-half**

5 cups **1% milk**, divided

1 cup **sugar**

12 **large egg yolks** (save the whites for Angel Food cake, Page 31)

1 cup **heavy cream**

½ cup **dark rum**

½ cup **brandy** or cognac

½ cup **bourbon**

1 pint **low-fat vanilla ice cream** (low-fat frozen vanilla yogurt is fine)

- In a medium saucepan, combine the half-and-half, 4 cups of milk, and sugar.
- Cook over low heat, stirring frequently, until the mixture reaches a slow simmer (bubbling around the edge but not boiling).
- In a medium bowl, whisk the egg yolks until combined. Very gradually whisk the hot mixture into the yolks. (Too much hot liquid at one time will cook the yolks.)
- Place the yolk mixture in the saucepan. Cook over low heat, stirring constantly with a wooden spoon, until the custard thickens and lightly coats the spoon. (An instant-read thermometer will read 180 degrees.)
- Cool the custard to room temperature. Cover with plastic wrap and refrigerate until very cold, 4 hours or overnight.
- When ready to serve the eggnog, whip the cream until soft peaks form. Gently fold the whipped cream into the chilled custard. Blend in the rum, cognac, and bourbon. If the eggnog seems too thick, it can be diluted with 1 cup of milk.
- Pour the eggnog into a punch bowl. Float the ice cream in the eggnog and serve in punch cups. This will keep the eggnog cold while serving.

Makes 20 servings. Each ½ cup serving supplies:
Calories(kcal) 235 Protein 5(g) Carbohydrates 19(g) Dietary Fiber 0(g) Cholesterol 158(mg) Fat 11(g) Sodium 58(mg)

[For as long as I can remember, I have served eggnog on Christmas Eve. When I learned about the danger of using raw eggs in eggnog, I was heartbroken, until I discovered this risk-free recipe, which cooks the egg yolks in a simple custard.]

Happy Birthday Chocolate Cake

This recipe came from a wonderful cook named Kay, who worked for us for many years. It promptly became our three children's favorite birthday cake – and was recently center stage at our first grandchild's first birthday!

- 2 cups **flour**
- 1¾ cup **sugar**
- ¾ cup **unsweetened cocoa**
- 2 tsp **baking soda**
- 1 tsp **baking powder**
- 1 tsp **salt**
- ½ cup **canola oil**
- 1 cup **milk** (low-fat is fine)
- 2 **large eggs**
- 1 cup **black coffee**, cold
- **Birthday Cake Frosting** (see below)

- Preheat oven to 350 degrees.
- In a large bowl, mix together all dry ingredients. Make a well in the middle and add the oil, milk, and eggs. Beat for 2 minutes with an electric mixer. Add the cold coffee and beat for an additional 2 minutes.

For a sheet cake: Pour the batter into 9-x-13-inch baking pan, greased and lightly floured. Bake for 40 to 45 minutes, until a toothpick comes out clean when inserted in cake. Cool cake in pan on a wire rack. Before frosting, cool cake completely (about 1 hour).
For a round layer cake: Divide the batter into 2 (9-inch) round cake pans and bake for 30 to 35 minutes. Cool the layers in the pans for 10 minutes, remove from pans and continue to cool on a wire rack.

Birthday Cake Frosting

While not purely healthy, this creamy frosting is made from scratch, from ingredients we all recognize. It's relatively low in sugar. And it's used to frost a birthday cake, which is far from a daily indulgence!

- 5 T **flour**
- 1 cup **1% milk**
- ½ cup **shortening**
- ½ cup **butter**, softened
- ¾ cup **sugar**
- 1 tsp **vanilla**

- Combine the milk and flour in a small saucepan. Cook over medium heat for about 5 minutes, until the mixture forms a thick paste. Be careful not to burn. Refrigerate until cold.
- In a medium bowl, cream the remaining ingredients. A little at a time, add the cooled paste, then beat the frosting with an electric mixer for 10 minutes.

Frosts one 9-by-13-inch sheet cake or two (9-inch) round layers.

Serves 16. Each serving (Cake with frosting) supplies::
Calories(kcal) 393 Protein 5(g) Carbohydrates 49(g) Dietary Fiber 1(g) Cholesterol 43(mg) Fat (20g) Sodium 399(mg)

Nutrient Analysis Information

The nutrient analysis for this cookbook has been provided by Nutrition and Food Solutions, LLC, owned and operated by Maria Wood, RD, LDN. Using Food Processor Software by ESHA Research, each recipe was analyzed for Calories, Protein, Carbohydrate, Dietary Fiber, Cholesterol, Fat and Sodium.

Each nutrient is rounded to the nearest whole number. Non-specific amounts i.e. "salt to taste", optional ingredients, and food used as garnishes or marinades, are not included in the calculation. When there is a range of ingredients i.e. "2-4 Tbsp" or serving size i.e. "4-6 servings," a mid-range value is calculated. If there is a choice of ingredients, i.e. "strawberries or peaches," the first food listed has been used in the calculation.

Nutrient data should be used and viewed as a guide, as there are many factors that affect the nutrient content of foods. Changing the amounts and types of food or the method of food preparation will change the data provided.

Maria is a Registered Dietitian who provides nutrition services including recipe and nutrient analysis, wellness nutrition, and food safety. She can be reached through her website, www.nutritionandfoodsolutions.com.

Index

NOTE: Page numbers in **bold** *indicate a photograph of the ingredient or recipe.*

C

D

E

F

G

H

I

K

L

M

N

O

P

Q

R

T

V

W

Y

Z